Dear Simon,

Happy Birthday!
(Please accept this out-size
                          card)

Love,
        Edward

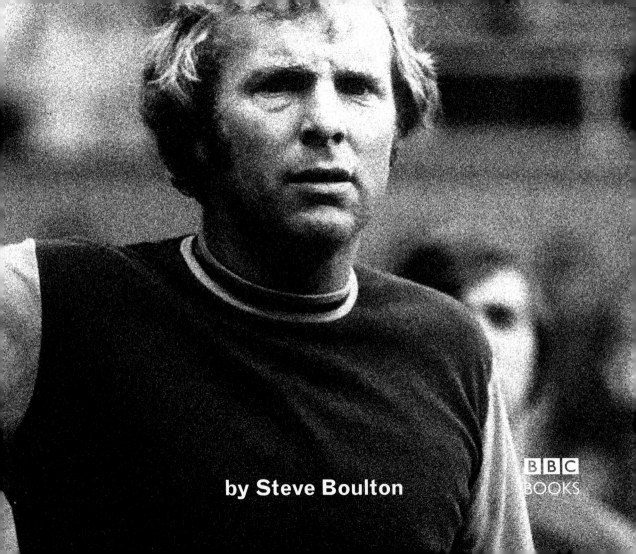

by **Steve Boulton**

BBC
BOOKS

Introduction

Thank you for taking the time to have a look at this compilation of wonderful cult heroes. First a few words to stop me getting an ear-bashing because your hero hasn't made the cut. Every single nominee and winner in this book was voted for by football fans. Whether it was via text, email or letters to *Football Focus*, whether it was via the **BBC** Sport website or your own individual club sites, what follows is down to many, many thousands of *your* votes. Thanks for getting as excited about the project as we did. I've used plenty of your comments in the book. They've been invaluable in bringing to life the stories of these remarkable characters.

So what makes a **Cult** Hero? Big hair, big tummy, big personality. All these are ways in. We've got players who are loved for a decade of dedication. We've also got those remembered for a single moment of magic ... or disaster!

In the book, four players have won for two different clubs. They're harder to guess than you'd imagine. Some players are nominated for a few clubs, but fail to win for any. To promote debate, we've put together our choice of a **Cult** Heroes **XI** at the end of the book – the ultimate team of fun. It's very much up for argument and we're planning a big *Football Focus* vote on *your* all-time cult side in the near future, so please keep watching every Saturday at 12.10 p.m. on **BBC1**. Email your larger-than-life side, made up of winners from this book, to *football@bbc.co.uk*.

Cult Heroes started as a simple idea to run on *Football Focus*, and in weeks had mushroomed into a debate across the land. *Football Focus*'s Assistant Editor, Shelley Alexander, has been tireless in her dedication to spread the word and to ensure justice is done at every club. I'd like to pay tribute to her and every one of our fantastic production staff on the programme. Everyone's played a part in some wonderful portrayals of our legends. Tony Gubba must also be singled out for his unwavering support from the off.

Thanks also to Viv at BBC Worldwide for her enthusiasm and making the book happen, Niall for his backing, Dee for all her hard work and encouragement, Steve for constantly improving the text, and everyone else involved in the design and production of this anoraks' delight. Special mention to Athers for making the website such a valuable part of *Football Focus*, Gilby for being such a top man, Suzz for being such a top woman, and Albert MBE for feeding us with all those facts for 37 years. Also thanks to Lawro for the terrible jokes, Manish, and all our pundits, reporters and commentators. Finally, thanks to Lou, Mum, Pat, Pete, Sue and all my family and friends for the kindness and reassurance that, unless I'm mistaken, has stopped me going even crazier than usual.

My all-time cult hero, by the way? Peter 'Swanny' Swan at Leeds. He tried so hard.

Hope you enjoy it.

Steve Boulton

Steve Boulton
Series Editor, *Football Focus*

To Dad & Vlad

This book has been published to accompany BBC1's
Football Focus, produced by BBC Television.
Series Editor: Steve Boulton, Series Producer: Andy Gilbert
Assistant Editor: Shelley Alexander

Published by BBC Books, BBC Worldwide Ltd,
Woodlands, 80 Wood Lane, London W12 0TT

First published in 2005
Copyright text © Steve Boulton 2005
The moral right of the author has been asserted.
For picture credits please see page 160

ISBN 0 563 52270 4

Commissioning Editor: Vivien Bowler
Project Editor: Deirdre O'Reilly
Designer: Bobby Birchall at DW Design
Copy-editor: Steve Dobell
Production Controller: Kenneth McKay

Set in Grotesque MT
Origination by Butler & Tanner Limited, Frome
Printed and bound in Italy by LEGO SpA

The Cult Heroes

Willie Miller 1971–90

Willie Miller was the captain of the most successful Aberdeen side in history. After joining the Dons as a 16-year-old, he went on to skipper Aberdeen during the period when Alex Ferguson managed the club. In 1983 Aberdeen shocked the footballing world by beating Real Madrid 2–1 to win the final of the European Cup Winners' Cup. If that was the pinnacle of Willie's playing achievements, it was certainly far from his only success. He led the club to three Scottish championships and four Scottish Cups, and he also won the European Super Cup. A majestic centre-back, Willie made his opinions known on the pitch: **'The fourth official before there ever was one. Willie told the refs what to do! He ran games without breaking sweat. His passion for the game and leadership on the park will never be beaten. His cult hero moment: scoring the goal against Celtic to clinch the championship in 1984. Captain Fantastic!'**

Willie also had a wonderful career with the national side, winning 65 caps for Scotland, as well as being voted into the greatest ever Scotland XI. Willie went on to become the manager of Aberdeen at the age of 36. Although they finished runners-up in the league twice and reached two cup finals, Willie failed to win silverware as boss. By his high standards, the club were deemed to have under-achieved and Willie moved into areas outside of football. Among other things, Willie now owns a Harry Ramsden's fish-and-chip shop franchise. As well as working for the BBC as a pundit, Willie returned to Pittodrie as executive football consultant in 2004. 'I can't think of anyone more deserving of cult hero status. Not only was he an inspiration on the pitch, he was worshipped by thousands off it. Had more than one opportunity to leave the club yet decided to stay. Now he's spearheading the revival of a club so dear to his and my heart.'

Owen Coyle 1990–93, 2001–02 & 2003–

No wonder **Owen Coyle** is a legend of **A**irdrie and their previous incarnation **Old Airdrieonians**. The striker, who was capped by Ireland and was born in Paisley, Scotland, has had three separate spells at the club. The one thing common to all three is his prolific scoring. **Owen** first joined **Old Airdrieonians** in 1990, notching up his first 50 goals for the club in three seasons. At this time in his life he wasn't averse to the odd transfer. He's had nine clubs in all, including Bolton, **D**umbarton and **M**otherwell. But he couldn't resist for ever. He returned in 2001 for a season, at the end of which he'd improved his scoring record for the club to better than a goal every other game. **Old Airdrieonians** finally bit the dust in 2002, and the old club's financial demise seemed to spell the end of the **Owen Coyle** association – but of course it didn't! He returned in November 2003 from **D**undee **U**nited and scored the goals that helped new club **A**irdrie win promotion to the **S**cottish First Divison.

Victor Kasule 1984–87

Victor Kasule lived a hedonistic lifestyle, and although the player nicknamed 'Vodka Vic' may not have fulfilled his potential on the pitch, he couldn't have received more adoration from the fans. As a player, Victor was once described by a newspaper as **'an armoured car of a winger with a cannon for a shot'**. Unfortunately he was a little too fond of a drink and this blighted his footballing success. Victor was from Glasgow. His mother was Scottish and his Dad was from Uganda. Those who watched Vic know that he had inherited immense natural talent. Meadowbank Thistle eventually bought him from Rovers for a club record transfer fee of £28,000 in 1987. Victor went through clubs the way he skipped past defenders. By the time he ran out of managers who would put up with his off-the-field ways, he'd played for the likes of Hamilton Academicals and Darlington as well as clubs in Finland, Malta and Ireland. **His scrapes included allegedly turning over a car belonging to another player – who didn't even know Vic was driving it.**

Steve 'Spider' Ramsay 1989–94 & 1997–99

Steve 'Spider' Ramsay was not big for a midfielder. However, he never let his size stop him from ruffling the feathers of the opposition. 'A neat player with an excellent touch and an eye for a pass. His slight build disguised the fact that he was willing to mix it with the best of them.' There was no doubt Spider could mix it! He was regularly suspended throughout his career, for making his presence felt, and ensuring his team stayed in control. In December 1998 after being sent off for a handball that he hotly disputed, it was reported that Steve called the ref a 'cheating wee ****!' As an influence on Alloa, his effect was immediate, the club clinching promotion to the first division in 1989. Not content with bossing the centre of the park, Steve weighed in with a respectable number of goals as well. In his final season he delighted the fans again as he helped Alloa to the third division title before finally leaving the Wasps for East Fife in 1999.

Craig Hinchcliffe 1995–2003

Questions have often been raised over the years about the quality of Scottish goalies, especially outside Scotland. But the fans of Arbroath believe they can help correct a few of the misconceptions. The 'Red Lichties' have been around since 1878 and in that time have weathered a fair few shots on goal. **They've chosen goalkeeper Craig Hinchcliffe as their all-time cult hero on the basis that he's one of the best stoppers they've ever seen.** Many a song has been sung in Hinchie's honour in the Tutties Neuk pub across the road from Arbroath's ground Gayfield. It all began after a tribunal decided that £11,000 would secure his transfer from Elgin City in July 1995. For the next eight years the Glaswegian threw himself around in the Arbroath cause with no regard for his own safety. It was with a heavy heart that he left for St Mirren in summer 2003 – but the sprightly spirit of Hinchie lives on.

Nominations Jimmy Bone **Craig Hinchcliffe** Andrew Penman

Tony Adams 1983–2002

Seaman, Dixon, Adams, Bould and Winterburn. The 'famous five' were the foundation of Arsenal's remarkable success in the late Eighties and Nineties. The most reliable defence of a generation, commanded by the most reliable footballing captain of a generation. Tony made his debut for the Gunners at the age of 17. Within two years, Arsenal's manager George Graham had taken the bold step of making his towering central defender the club's captain. The responsibility was carried well, and in 1987 Tony lifted the League Cup after his side defeated Liverpool. In the same year, Tony won his first England cap in the 4–2 win over Spain in Madrid. He was also voted the PFA Young Player of the Year by his peers. Then came one of the most remarkable league championship finishes in history. It was 1989 and the final match of the season was Liverpool versus Arsenal at Anfield. Arsenal needed to win by two clear goals to snatch the title away from the Merseyside club. Tony's side were a goal ahead going into stoppage time when Michael Thomas stole the most dramatic winner to the delight of the travelling support and large swathes of North London. From the outside, life appeared to be perfect for Tony, but then at Christmas 1990 the public perception changed. Tony was jailed for drink driving. He was released a couple of months later, in time to lead Arsenal to their second championship in three years, but there was an underlying problem. After captaining England to the semi-finals of Euro '96, Tony went on a drinking binge that would change him for ever. By the end of it, Tony realised he had to reform his life if he was ever to be happy. He sought help and admitted to his alcoholism. **'Tony went through personal difficulties in the public eye and emerged deserving nothing but respect. A legend.'** The sober Tony went on to win the League and FA Cup double in 1998 and 2002 with Arsenal, now under manager Arsène Wenger. His 669th and final appearance for Arsenal was in the 2–0 FA Cup final win in 2002 against Chelsea. In his time, Arsenal also won a League Cup and FA Cup double in 1993 as well as the European Cup Winners' Cup in 1994. Tony is the founder of the successful charity Sporting Chance, which helps sports men and women to overcome their addiction problems.

Paul McGrath 1989–96

Nominations Gordon Cowans **Paul McGrath** Nigel Spink

Virtually every Aston Villa fan would agree that Paul McGrath is a miracle of science. Throughout his career he was beset with terrible knee problems that required eight operations, in all, to keep him mobile. Often he was hardly able to train, just performing on match days. On top of that, Paul has struggled against an alcohol problem that often led him into trouble on and off the pitch. Despite his problems, he is worshipped by the Villa Park faithful. 'He came to us with dodgy knees and the reputation as a drinker. He went on to perform brilliantly in every match he played for Villa.' Paul joined the Midlands club in 1989. Alex Ferguson thought he was a bad influence at Manchester United, and so he sold him to Villa for £400,000. That was in August. By Boxing Day, Paul's new side had proved a point, beating Man Utd 3–0. Villa went on to finish the season as runners-up to Liverpool in the league, as well as reaching the quarter-finals of the FA Cup. The fans were soon chanting their tribute song, 'Ooh Aah Paul McGrath, I said Ooh Aah Paul McGrath!' In 1993, Villa again finished runners-up in the league. Paul was awarded the PFA's Footballer of the Year award. This went alongside his Villa player of the year gong, which he had won for four years on the trot. **1994 brought a fantastic moment for Paul. Villa reached the League Cup final. Their opponents?** Who else, of course, but Fergie's men. **Paul was suffering from a shoulder injury, but there was no way he was going to miss out on the chance of putting one over the man who had sold him. Villa took the trophy, beating United 3–1. Next up, Paul headed for the USA for the World Cup with the Republic of Ireland team. In their opening game, Ireland stunned Italy with a 1–0 victory. Ireland eventually went out to Holland, but the legendary defender Franco Baresi said that he believed Paul was the best defender in the world. This, of course, was something that Villa fans believed they knew already.** Paul ended up with 83 international caps. Before leaving for Derby in 1996, Paul put in another masterful display as Villa beat Leeds 3–0 to win the League Cup final again.

Hugh Sproat 1974–79 & 1984–86

Hugh Sproat is a legend at Somerset Park. The goalkeeper was one of these people who just wouldn't be fazed by anything. Fellow team-

mates remember him always running late for training and yet somehow getting to where he needed to be just in the nick of time. Hugh was also a fine keeper for Ayr. He saved his beloved side on many occasions and left opposition strikers in no doubt as to who was in command of the penalty box. He also enjoyed 'winding up' the opposition. Any psychological edge would be taken. 'Hughie would wear a green jersey when he was playing against Rangers, and a blue one when he was up against Celtic! He loved a bit of banter with the opposition fans.' Hugh was certainly a great eccentric. 'He was a bit of a punk rocker really. He tried to get away with wearing a razor blade in his ear during games. An extrovert and a brilliant all-round goalie.'

Ronnie Glavin 1979–85

'A terrier in strength and determination – he never gave up,' says one Barnsley fan. Ronnie Glavin was a firm favourite at Oakwell. A goalscoring midfielder, he began his South Yorkshire career in 1979 after he joined Barnsley from Celtic for a then record club fee of £50,000. Ronnie also played for Partick Thistle, Stockport and Portuguese side Belenenses, before finishing his playing career in the USA. Later Ronnie actually returned to Barnsley for a short spell as first-team coach. This was after a lower-league managerial career which started with Frickley and moved on to Emley, culminating in a memorable FA Cup run which brought a third-round tie at West Ham in 1998. In his playing days the little Scotsman signalled the start of better times at Barnsley, and his attitude is still revered by the supporters today. Another fan perhaps sums him up best of all. **'A maestro of the midfield in the Eighties. Ronnie made us feel that anything was possible.'**

Nominations **Ronnie Glavin** Mick McCarthy Clint Marcelle

Jock Wallace 1956–58 & 1965–68

Jock Wallace returned to Berwick Rangers as player/manager in 1965 and a season or so later he had an integral part to play in the club's finest hour. It was 1967 and they were playing Glasgow Rangers in the cup. At full time viewers in Scotland heard the TV presenter famously announce, 'We have a scoreline from Shielfield Park in Berwick. Hold on, this can't be right! We'll have this corrected! It says **Berwick 1, Rangers 0.'** The result was 100 per cent correct. This wasn't Jock's first giant-killing, however. He was a goalkeeper who liked to be knocking about between the sticks when a shock was on the cards. In 1964 he helped to humiliate all self-respecting Geordies. Forget Ronnie Radford's scorcher that led to Hereford humbling the Toon in the Seventies. Bedford Town knocked Newcastle out of the FA Cup a decade before that, with Jock keeping them at bay. After his second spell at Berwick this Scottish legend went on to train, then manage Glasgow Rangers, leading them to European Cup Winners' Cup success and two domestic trebles in the Seventies.

Trevor Francis 1969–79

Birmingham City

Nominations Steve Claridge **Trevor Francis** Frank Worthington

Trevor Francis joined the Blues as an apprentice in July 1969 and he had not yet turned professional by the time he made his debut just over a year later at the age of 16. That first game was against Cardiff City at Ninian Park, but the highlight of Trevor's first season came when he scored all four goals in a win over Bolton – the first 16-year-old to achieve such a scoring feat. Trevor was also a member of the Birmingham youth side that reached the quarter-finals of the FA Youth Cup in 1970–71. The good-looking youngster had everything – pace, touch and an ability to conjure up a goal from nowhere. He could also cross a ball with deadly accuracy. In 1972 he helped the team to promotion into the top division. He was also a key player as Birmingham reached the FA Cup semi-finals on two occasions in 1972 and 1975. In 1977 Trevor made his England debut, winning the first of 51 caps. A year later, he decided to play for Detroit Express in the USA. This was in the American soccer season, on top of his English fixtures for City. In 1979 he became the first £1 million player when he joined Brian Clough's Nottingham Forest. Trevor scored the only goal in that season's European Cup final as Forest beat Malmo of Sweden. Trevor went on to play for Manchester City, Sampdoria, Atalanta, Rangers, QPR and Sheffield Wednesday. Later he pursued a career in management, which included bossing the Blues from 1996 to 2001.

Simon Garner 1978–92

'A face like a bag of spanners but as graceful a player as you're ever likely to see.' The Blackburn fans love Simon Garner. You realise how much when you think about the other players they could have chosen as their all-time cult hero. Notably Alan Shearer and Colin Hendry. What they seem to admire most is the rumour among the crowd that Simon would have a fag at half-time to steady himself in front of goal for the second half. He's also described as 'the Kenny Dalglish of the lower leagues'. Born in Boston, he was nicknamed 'the Lincolnshire Poacher' – and for very good reason. He is the club's all-time record scorer with nearly 200 goals over 14 years. He only left when Jack Walker's millions allowed the superstars, and the Premiership, to arrive at Ewood Park. A man of the people, often seen going for a drink with the fans after the game, he went on to become a painter and decorator.

Alan Suddick 1966–76

Known as 'the King' at Blackpool, Alan entranced the Bloomfield Road crowd with his skill in midfield. Previously he had been an idol on Tyneside, scoring 41 times in 144 appearances for Newcastle before signing for Blackpool for £63,000. In no time at all he had convinced the crowd he could do virtually anything with the ball. 'Never mind Beckham, this man could bend a ball round a wall from any distance. As soon as Blackpool gained a free-kick near the box the cry used to go up: "It's going to be a Suddick bender." He had great skill and was the King for most of the Seventies.' Alan was also the greatest exponent of 'keepy uppies' that anyone had seen. With his touch he could keep the ball in the air as long as he wanted. He masterminded the 2–1 victory over Bologna in the Anglo-Italian Cup final in 1971. After his playing career finished he went on to set up a decorating business in Blackpool.

Nat Lofthouse 1946–61

If you thought the comedian Peter Kay was the biggest thing to come out of Bolton, you're way off the mark. Nat Lofthouse holds that honour in a town where he was born, where he played his football and where he spent his whole life. During the Forties and Fifties Bolton were top of the football ladder and the place took 'Lofty' to its heart. He in turn couldn't have loved his home more. He once wrote a dedication ' ... to the people of Bolton. Without you none of this would have been possible.' Nat became known as 'the Lion of Vienna' for his international exploits. In 1952 England were drawing 2–2 in Austria when Nat ran the length of the pitch and was clattered senseless by the keeper while scoring the winner – his second of the game. It didn't stop his England team-mates taking the mickey. 'Eddie Baily (Spurs) always used to ask me why I wasn't wearing clogs and a flat cap! They were having a laugh but it hurt. I was proud to come from Bolton. I don't think there's a nicer sight anywhere than our Town Hall Square.' Nat's roles at the club since his playing days have included those of club president, manager, trainer, coach and chief scout.

Paul 'Bazza' Bastock 1992–2004

'Bazza' Bastock is a legend between the sticks in Lincolnshire. He made saves throughout Boston's rise into the Football League and ended up with the club's all-time appearances record, his incredible tally of 625 games eclipsing Billy Howells' earlier record of 572.

Paul started out with Coventry City, where he won the FA Youth Cup in 1987. After spells with Cambridge Utd and Malaysian club Sabah, Paul joined the Pilgrims from Kettering Town in August 1992. He helped Boston climb from the Northern Premier League, via the Dr Martens League and the Conference, to their ultimate goal, a place in Football League Division Three, in 2002. Paul then boasted a 100 per cent appearance record in United's first two league seasons as they consolidated their place in the division. 'We all adore Paul so much. He just couldn't do enough for the club. So much so, he ended up marrying the Chairman's daughter!' Paul was voted Boston's player of the year in 1992–93 and again ten years later in 2002–03. He was granted a testimonial year in 2000–01.

Nominations **Paul Bastock** Chris Cook Paul Ellender

Nominations **Steve Fletcher** Ted MacDougall Sean O'Driscoll

Steve Fletcher 1992–

Steve Fletcher is a proper centre-forward. Big and strong. He's spent well over a decade up front for the Cherries, so the fans know what to expect from him. 'He's the best, worst player in the world (if that makes sense!). He's tall but has one of the worst strike rates ever. Little more than a goal every five games. So many of his goals have been "shinned in" and he may have a head like a 50p coin (you don't know which way the ball will bounce off), but we just don't seem to be able to win without him!' In April 2005, Steve passed 500 games for Bournemouth. He was touched when his team-mates presented him with a specially framed memento of the occasion which they'd all clubbed together for. He then broke the club's all-time appearances record, previously held by his manager Sean O'Driscoll. Steve's greatest moment came in the 2003 play-off final at Cardiff. A long, upfield punt came to Steve and in an instant he hooked in the opening goal of the game. It set up the biggest winning margin in a play-off final. The 5–2 win over Lincoln City took Bournemouth into Division Two.

Stuart McCall touched the hearts of Bradford fans in many ways. They love his red hair. They love the fact that when he left the club for the first time in 1988 he said he had 'unfinished business' at Bradford and that he'd return. He was true to his word. Bradford fans also love the fact that Stuart fell off a car bonnet while celebrating promotion to the Premiership! 'He was the heart and soul at Valley Parade in times of triumph and tragedy,' wrote one. The tragedy of course was the Bradford fire that so cruelly took the lives of 56 fans in 1985. Another fan remembers, 'Stuart nearly lost his Dad in the fire, irrevocably putting him side by side with the rest of us who were there that day.' Away from Bradford, Stuart scored twice after coming on as a substitute in the 1989 FA Cup final for Everton against Liverpool. He still ended up on the losing side. But City fans remember Stuart as theirs.

Ian Campbell 1977–84

For nearly 80 years Brechin City had never been higher than the Scottish second division. To many that seemed like a long, long time to suffer nothing much but bad seasons with the odd mediocre campaign thrown in. But then in 1983 they won the league and went into Division One for the very first time. The man who'd been scoring a vast share of their goals for the past six seasons was Ian Campbell. Nicknamed 'Pink', because he used to run like the Pink Panther, Ian eventually became the club's all-time leading scorer, but it wasn't always that way. He began at Brechin as a midfielder, and what a waste it could have been if his true talent hadn't been spotted. Thankfully, he was given a try up front and netted 20-plus goals most seasons before leaving to join Dunfermline Athletic. In January 2005 'Pink' took over from his twin brother, Dick, as manager of Brechin. Dick had moved to Partick Thistle and a month later they both won manager of the month awards for their respective clubs. A unique achievement.

Terry Evans 1985–93

'Big Tel' was a giant of a player in every sense. Six foot five inches tall, Terry commanded the centre of defence for the Bees for eight years. He was also the club captain and he led them to the 1992 Division Three championship. One trademark was his powering presence in the air, as a fan recalls: **'I witnessed him heading the ball from box to box on more than one occasion! If you cut him he'd bleed red and white.'** Terry had arrived from non-league Hillingdon Borough for £5,000. By the time he was signed by Wycombe in 1993 his value had risen to £40,000. Although he'd left Brentford, the fans at Griffin Park continued to have a soft spot for Terry. **'Even after he'd scored for Wycombe against us, our fans still sang "There's only one Terry Evans." A true legend.'**

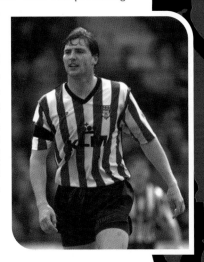

Nominations **Terry Evans** Dean Holdsworth Terry Hurlock

Peter Ward 1975–80 & 1982–83

'He shot, he scored, it must be Peter Ward ... Peter Ward!' The song sums up how the fans at the Goldstone Ground felt about their goalscoring hero. Originally a plane engine fitter for Rolls-Royce, Peter made a supersonic impression at Brighton. He was just 50 seconds into his debut game when he scored the first of the 95 goals he finally bagged for the Seagulls. 'Whizz' was his nickname, and although he was not always considered the most industrious player, no-one doubted his skill and finishing. His club record 36 goals in the 1976–77 season helped Brighton win promotion from the third division. He then scored a hat-trick on his debut for England Under 21s against Norway at the Goldstone. The next season he was leading scorer at Brighton again as they won promotion to the top flight. After helping the club to consolidate their position in Division One, Peter was finally signed by Brian Clough and Peter Taylor for Nottingham Forest for £400,000. He returned for a short loan spell before moving to America.

Dariusz 'Jacki' Dziekanowski 1992–94

'Jacki' Dziekanowski was a true fans' favourite at Ashton Gate. He was not at Bristol City for that long, and even when he was, he would often start on the bench, but to City fans he was a star. 'Jacki remains to this day the most entertaining forward player I have ever seen in a Bristol City shirt. To further endear him to me, he had a reputation for living life to the full!' Jacki, a Polish international, arrived at the club from Celtic in 1992 for a quarter of a million pounds. On the pitch he performed tricks for fun. Off it, he enjoyed the nightlife, and although West Country cider was probably not his drink of choice, Jacki was well known around town. **'Made Gazza look like a choirboy and yet Jacki's still the most outrageously gifted City player I've ever seen.'** Russell Osman was player-manager at Bristol City and took the unpopular decision to get rid of him. He allowed Jacki one final match in front of the home fans, and before the game, Jacki was paraded to tumultuous applause. Russell Osman then scored during the match, but when his name was announced on the tannoy, he was roundly booed by City fans, devastated that their hero was being forced to leave.

Ian Holloway 1981–85, 1987–91 & 1996–2000

Three spells at Bristol Rovers as a player, combined with nearly five years as manager of the Club, secured Ian Holloway the Bristol Rovers cult hero award.

'He typified what Gasheads think "being Gas" is all about. Spirit, determination and not a bad player either. Hated losing, hated City – which was always going to endear him to those of us who live on the right side of the river!' The rivalry with Bristol City is fierce, and Ian was with Rovers in 1990 when the third division championship came down to a derby game between the two clubs at the end of the season. Two goals from Devon White helped Rovers claim the title and put one over on their deadly foe. **'I watched "Ollie" as a player-manager and he brought belief back to the club and was the most passionate** person I have ever seen at Bristol Rovers during my years watching. He was proud to manage and play for Bristol Rovers and made me and so many others proud to be a Gashead.' Ian has a very positive outlook on life. He has also carved out a niche as a comedy genius.

His post-match interviews are littered with David Brent-isms. These started in Bristol and have moved on to **QPR**, where he was appointed manager in 2001. Perhaps the most famous of them goes as follows: 'To put it in gentleman's terms. If you've been out for a night and you're looking for a young lady and you pull one, some weeks they're good-looking and some weeks they're not the best. Our performance today would have not been the best-looking bird, but at least we got her in the taxi. She weren't the best-looking lady we ended up taking home, but she was very pleasant and very nice, so thanks very much, let's have a coffee.'

Burnley

Jimmy McIlroy 1950–63

Jimmy McIlroy was one of the great inside-forwards. He came to England from Glentoran in Northern Ireland. **He was just 18 years old and cost manager Frank Hill £8,000.** However, it was under manager Harry Potts that he had his most successful period. Burnley had won the English title in 1921. In the subsequent four decades they had spent a significant period in the second division and looked unlikely to achieve the same success again. But in 1959–60 all that was to change. Jimmy's role would be seen as a midfield position nowadays, and yet he still scored at a prolific rate. His goals and ability meant that a win in Burnley's last game of the season, away to Manchester City, would give the Clarets the first division title. Burnley went 1–0 up before Man City equalised. Trevor Meredith restored Burnley's lead and the team clung on to win the championship. The next season, which saw them playing in the European Cup, they reached the FA Cup and League Cup semi-finals. Then, in 1962, as well as finishing runners-up in the league, Burnley fans had a day out at Wembley before losing the FA Cup final 3–1 to Spurs. The next year Jimmy left Burnley to go to Stoke, however he missed the town so much that he returned and still lives there. At Turf Moor they have named a stand in his honour.

Craig Madden 1977–86

Craig Madden is Bury's all-time record-holder for goalscoring. In a nine-year period 'Charlie' managed to notch up 149 goals in 336 games and win many thousands of Gigg Lane hearts. **'Craig was the first God to grace Bury's turf. A bit like Van Nistelrooy, always there in the box to fire home the winner ... usually in the last few minutes.'** Craig joined Bury from Northern Nomads on a free transfer. He scored 10 goals in the 1979–80 season to secure a regular first-team place, and from then on he was on fire. In 1981–82 he scored a remarkable 42 league and cup goals in 52 games. In the league his 35 strikes earned him the Golden Boot for being England's top scorer. During his career, Craig had two particularly fruitful strike partnerships – first with Stevie Johnson, then with Wayne Entwhistle. It was with 'Enty' that Craig grabbed the goals that secured promotion for Bury into Division Three in 1984–85.

Nominations David Adekola Greg Farrell **Craig Madden**

35

Nominations Alan Biley Lionel Perez Lindsay Smith

Lindsay 'Wolfie' Smith 1977–82 & 1986–89

Every now and again you get a cult hero who might not have been **George Best** in talent, but who the crowd can't fail to fall in love with. Every now and again you get a cult hero with a cracking nickname and every now and again you get a cult hero who all the fans, young and old, seem to want to email us about. Step forward and take a bow **Mr Lindsay 'Wolfie' Smith.** 'Simply awesome, he could hoof the ball with finesse.'

A true **Seventies** and early **Eighties** man, **Lindsay** was hard. The chant at the **Abbey Stadium** was 'Lindsay's gonna get yer' – and he did. **Often.** He once got booked when one of his team-mates played a long back-pass to him. Lindsay trapped the ball, then just sat on it and gestured the opposition striker to come and get it. Last sighting by a fan is described as follows. 'I saw him in a chip shop in **Cambridge** looking as lean and as menacing as ever. Cracking blonde curly hair and moustache slightly too close in image to a German porn star (male that is).' Thanks for the clarification.

umbro

Having already been voted Reading's all-time cult hero for the couple of seasons he burned brightly at Elm Park, Robin moved on to Cardiff. The combination of his chaotic lifestyle and his magnificent football continued at full pelt. The Welsh fans, just like the Reading fans, fell for the lovable rogue. **'A genius of dubious temperament,'** wrote one fan. **'Famous for his hat-trick against Luton where, having just scored a great goal, he flashed a V-sign to the distraught goalkeeper as the ball hit the back of the net.'** The photograph of this moment was subsequently used on the sleeve of the Super Furry Animals record, *The Man Don't Give a F*ck*. The truth was that Robin didn't – at least not for his own well-being. After Cardiff, his career and life spiralled together into non-league football, illness and a death that everyone who saw this enigma agrees was far, far too early.

Henrik Larsson 1997–2004

The sight of Henrik Larsson sticking his tongue out could not have made Celtic fans happier. It normally happened after he'd found the back of the net, and it became the super-scoring Swede's trademark. Henrik joined the Glasgow club in 1997 from Feyenoord. In hindsight, his £650,000 transfer fee was one of the all-time footballing bargains. 242 goals in 315 games is a phenomenal record by anyone, in any era. He was a bit shaky to start with, but scored 16 times as Celtic took

the league title in his first season. The following campaign brought goals, but saw Celtic lose out to Rangers in the league. Things got even worse in the 1999–2000 season. After a promising start, Henrik suffered a horrific leg break during a UEFA Cup tie against Lyon. Remarkably, he made a swift recovery but then injured his leg again. Despite virtually no match practice, he was called up for Sweden at Euro 2000. He was lacking fitness but still managed to score against Italy. The Swedes, however, finished bottom of their group. When Martin O'Neill arrived to take charge at Celtic, Henrik's fortunes dramatically improved. He scored a staggering 52 goals in all competitions as Celtic completed a domestic treble. To cap it all, a year or so after his career had looked to be threatened, Henrik was presented with the European Golden Shoe in recognition of his incredible goal-scoring feats. The goals, awards and trophies kept coming until Henrik decided 2004 would be his final season at Celtic. He scored twice late on to secure a 2–1 victory for his beloved club in his final competitive game for them. Henrik wept in front of his adoring fans at the final whistle. 'The man was praised as a Ghod (that h is intentional!). He didn't seem to succumb to any prima donna ways and is the only man I've seen reduce 60,000 grown brutes of men to tears.' After scoring three goals for Sweden at Euro 2004 he was signed by Spanish giants Barcelona.

Clive Mendonca 1997–2002

He was nicknamed 'Super Clive' by the fans, and Clive Mendonca's arrival at the Valley marked a rise in the team's recent fortunes. £700,000 was the cost of Clive from Grimsby where he was also voted Cult Hero. He'd previously had spells at Sheffield United, Doncaster Rovers and Rotherham. Although he suffered terrible injury setbacks, Clive's goalscoring record at Charlton stands at more than a goal every other game. For the fans of any club, there is normally one game that stands out above all others as the greatest they have ever witnessed. Those who watched, fascinated, the 1998 first division play-off final between Charlton and Sunderland could claim with some justification that they saw the most entertaining game ever played at Wembley. Clive Mendonca was the star of the show. He put Charlton ahead and then helped them to stay in the game after intense Sunderland pressure. By full time it was 3–3. By the end of extra time Clive had collected a hat-trick and it was 4–4. So it went to penalties. The free scoring continued until, at 7–6 to

Charlton, Sasa Ilic saved from Michael Gray. Clive had beaten the team he supported as a kid and confirmed himself as an all-time Valley hero. Charlton were in the Premiership. 'The greatest football match in the history of the world! Clive was simply magnificent. After that performance I would have done anything he asked. I think that pretty much goes for every single Charlton fan there is!' Eventually Clive was told that if he played on, it would mean he'd have to have his hip replaced at some point. His last competitive game for Charlton was just before the turn of the millennium, but the club stood by him until he finally decided it was time to quit in 2002. The following year he was the popular recipient of a benefit match against NEC Nijmegen. Clive was offered a coaching role by Charlton, but turned it down to return to his native North-East with his family.

Gianfranco Zola 1996–2003

'Probably the best player I've ever seen and certainly the best foreign player ever to play in the English league. An artist and a gentleman. Irreplaceable.' Gianfranco Zola inspired Chelsea fans like no other player. He never gave less than his best and often dazzled the crowd with his wonderful skills. The five-foot, six-inch Italian arrived from Parma for £4.5 million in November 1996. He played with a smile and he played with panache, bringing balls down on the turn, riding tackles and running at the opposition – causing mayhem. He could also strike a mean free-kick. His work-rate was phenomenal and he was well known for training long after other players had gone home. He also helped bring trophies to Stamford Bridge. In 1997 it was his mid-air back-heel that allowed Eddie Newton to make it 2–0 in the FA Cup final win over Middlesbrough. The League Cup followed – again with a 2–0 victory over Boro – and Chelsea went on to reach the final of the European Cup Winners' Cup in 1998. Before the final, against Stuttgart, Gianfranco had been injured and so started the game on the bench. In the 71st minute, with the game goalless, Gianfranco was brought on. Within 30 seconds he'd fired home a cracking winner and secured Chelsea their first European silverware for 27 years. The club then won the European Super Cup, the 2000 FA Cup final, beating Aston Villa 1–0 – the goal coming after a goalkeeper fumble from

Gianfranco's free-kick – and also the Charity Shield of the same year. Six trophies came in all during his time at the club. At the age of 36 Gianfranco played his final game for Chelsea – against Liverpool. Brought on near the end, he sparkled for one last time in a 2–1 victory. At the final whistle he was applauded off by both sets of fans. When Roman Abramovich then arrived at Chelsea, he was so impressed by the Italian that he tried to lure him to stay at Stamford Bridge. However, Gianfranco insisted that he'd promised his hometown club, Cagliari in Sardinia, that he'd sign for them, and he refused to break his word. Fittingly, he led them to promotion into Serie A the following season. Soon after, Gianfranco was awarded an honorary **OBE** for services to English football.

Neil Grayson 1998–2002

Neil **G**rayson came to the club at which he wins his cult hero status at the tender age of 33! **B**rought in to score goals, he certainly netted at a respectable rate. **B**ut the **W**haddon **R**oad faithful didn't fall for him on talent alone. **H**e was the most committed player that **R**obins fans had ever seen. '**A**fter a few seasons of passionate displays, **N**eil totally endeared himself to everyone at the club. **A** monster on the pitch, but a gentleman and a family man off it.' **N**eil was part of the **S**teve **C**otterill era, when the club waved goodbye to non-league status, and it was fitting that he played his last game at the **M**illennium **S**tadium. **H**e came on as a sub and hit the post near the end of the 3–1 victory over **R**ushden & **D**iamonds in the 2002 play-off final. **T**he victory meant that after three promotions in five years, **C**heltenham moved into **D**ivision **T**wo.

Grenville Millington 1969 & 1973–83

Grenville Millington was a loyal and dependable goalkeeper for Chester (in Grenville's day the club had not added the City to their name). **He won the club's player of the season award on three occasions and was between the sticks when they beat the league champions Leeds 3–0 on the way to the semi-final of the League Cup as a fourth division side in 1975.** These credentials alone could have secured the Chester all-time cult hero award, but there is another event for which Grenville will always be remembered. It came in a League Cup match in 1981 at Sealand Road. The opponents were Plymouth Argyle. With 12 minutes of the tie remaining, the score was locked at 2–2. Argyle striker David Kemp got his head to a cross and, as the ball flew towards the net, Grenville launched his burly figure towards it. He couldn't reach it, but he did manage to crash into the post, snapping it and in the process demolishing the goal. Grenville was dazed. The game was abandoned with the Plymouth striker still claiming the ball had crossed the line and that the goal should stand – even if the goalposts didn't!

Chester City

Nominations Gary Bennett Grenville Millington Ian Rush

Ernie Moss 1968–76, 1979–81 & 1984–86

Ernie Moss had some stiff competition to bag the all-time 'Spires' cult hero gong. One of his chief competitors, Bob Newton, has gone nude in a calendar to raise money to help the fight against breast cancer. Another, Jamie Hewitt, scored the equalising goal in the gripping 1997 FA Cup semi-final with Middlesbrough. But Ernie beat them both off, on the strength of his goals ... and his love of the club. He's Chesterfield's record goalscorer with 162 goals in 469 appearances between 1968 and 1986. **'Our fans can't get enough of Ernie. He was part of the side that won the fourth division in 1970 and we don't forget!'** Ernie went on to run a sports shop in the town and has been manager of a number of non-league teams, most successfully at near neighbours Matlock Town. He also has another little sideline. He can sometimes be heard as an expert summariser on a local radio sports show called *Back of the Net*.

Clyde's second division championship win in 1978 is fondly remembered by all Clyde fans of the era. No-one came closer to personifying the team's spirit in those days than Neilly Hood. He has been described as 'a scorer with attitude – he hit them from anywhere and they usually went in!' Yes, this was a player who wasn't content with a tap-in. Neilly wanted the fans to remember his goals. There were 76 for the club in the seven years after he joined in 1975, so he gave himself plenty of chances to register a belter. He was no shrinking violet either. 'One of the bravest players I've ever seen in a Clyde jersey. He would run through a brick wall for you and had a great rapport with the fans.' That connection with the fans carries on to this day. Neilly Hood makes his presence felt in the hospitality suites at Broadwood on match days. He's always happy to recall Clyde's great seasons ... and of course a few of the finishes that helped the club to success.

Lomano LuaLua 1998–2000

Colchester not only claims to be England's oldest recorded town – it also claims to have launched the career of the most talented footballer ever to emerge from the Democratic Republic of Congo. Lomano LuaLua – 'so good they named him twice' – didn't play in the first team for very long. Much of his fame was won by coming off the bench and putting in match-winning supersub performances. 'Invariably confused himself more than the opposition ... scored a hat-trick in his final game for the U's that will stick in the mind for ever. Dropped shoulders, incredible dribbling and cheeky flicks. All done with a permanent smile on his face.' Here was a man who apparently played purely for the love of the game. He also earned a tidy £2.25 million for the Essex club when Bobby Robson took a chance signing him for Newcastle United. 'Breathtaking skills all capped off with his trademark over-the-top somersaults once he found the net!'

David Speedie 1987–91

'Fiery' is a word which crops up a lot when sky-blue fans describe David Speedie. Bought with money earned by Coventry's 1987 FA Cup victory, Speedie was never slow to put himself about on and off the pitch. He was a real favourite who always gave 100 per cent. Away fans hated this Scotsman who was born in Glenrothes. One supporter recalls: **'A Hammers fan once said to me, "I detest that Speedie with a passion ... but I'd have him on our team any day!"'** This summed the man up. He scored some memorable goals. Audacious lobs and great headers were his specialities. David played for many clubs in his career including Chelsea, Liverpool and Blackburn. He was so adaptable that he could slot in up front and start scoring goals from the off. He eventually left Coventry in a move to Anfield in 1991.

Nominations Keith Houchen Mick Quinn **David Speedie**

49

Craig Levein 1981–83

Cowdenbeath are known as 'the blue Brazil', so their fans were always likely to recognise class above all else when selecting their all-time cult hero. Craig Levein joined the club in 1981 at the age of 17. Another of Cowdenbeath's nominations, Andy Rolland, was the man who signed him. As a centre-back, he swiftly made an impression on the fans. 'Surely the best defender the club has had, even though he only played one and a half seasons for us as a teenager.' Craig left in 1983 to play for Hearts. His outstanding career included Hearts' infamous 1985–86 season. The club looked set for a remarkable league and cup double, but Craig picked up a flu bug and missed the last league game of the season. Hearts went down 2–1, losing the league title in the process. They also lost in the Cup final to Aberdeen shortly after. Craig could be fiery and once received a 14-game ban for punching a team-mate. He gained 16 caps for Scotland and played in the 1990 World Cup. When he returned to Cowdenbeath as manager in 1997, the club were languishing in Scottish Division Three. By the time Craig was snapped up again by Hearts in 2000, 'the blue Brazil' were on their way to a rare promotion.

Seth Johnson

Seth Johnson stole the hearts of the fans at Gretsy Road by choosing not to leave the club when they were in trouble. His combative style had already made him a firm favourite when Derby County came waving the big bucks about. Here was an ambitious young man who many were talking about as a future England international (Seth does in fact have a cap). He decided that he didn't want to desert his colleagues in their time of need and so he held off on a £3 million move until after the season was done. In what time he had left at the club, he helped Dario Gradi's men beat the drop by scoring the important winning goal against Bristol City. The cash from his eventual departure provided a much-needed boost for the Alex. Seth went on to an even bigger move when he was sold for £7 million to Leeds United, where according to rumour the club insisted they wouldn't pay the earth for the player and subsequently offered Seth twice the weekly wage he'd been expecting!

Nominations Craig Hignett **Seth Johnson** Danny Murphy

Crewe Alexandra

Crystal Palace

Ian Wright 1985–91

Nominations Attilio Lombardo Peter Taylor Ian Wright

The fans should be allowed to kick off our description of Ian Wright. 'The best Palace striker ever. Along with Mark Bright the greatest combination the Eagles have ever had.' 'Ian Wright is an excitable, energetic bag of entertainment!' An unusual description of a person but, it has to be said, pretty apt. The truth with Ian Wright is that he loves meeting people and having fun.

In his first season at Selhurst Park Ian was often used as a supersub and still managed to end up as Palace's second top scorer. Once the Wrighty and Brighty combination kicked into action things got even better. In 1989 their goals pushed the club into the play-offs and then to promotion to the first division. Wrighty then grabbed 27 goals to break the club's record for a player in one season in the top flight. If one moment could sum up a man who was one of the game's most ruthless scorers ever,

it would have to be the 1990 FA Cup final against Manchester United. Ian had been suffering for some while after cracking a shin bone. He missed the epic 4–3 semi-final win over Liverpool, but he was so desperate to play at Wembley that manager Steve Coppell put him on the bench. With time running out and Palace losing 2–1, Wright was brought on for a last-ditch effort. Within minutes he'd screamed into the United penalty area, tricked the defence and slotted the equaliser. He got another in extra time, and only a late Mark Hughes goal made it 3–3 and stopped the unthinkable happening. Palace lost a tight replay 1–0. The following season Ian got his first England cap and also helped the club to win the Zenith Data Systems Cup final at Wembley. He scored twice as Palace beat Everton. Wrighty then moved on to Arsenal, where he broke their all-time goalscoring record, but the Selhurst Park faithful will always consider him one of theirs.

Craig Liddle 1998–

When Craig Liddle captained Darlington against Swansea at the end of the 2004 season he became one of an élite band of players to have played 300 games for the Quakers. It was another milestone for the committed defender in a career journey that began as a trainee at Aston Villa. Craig didn't break through at Villa, and so he spent a few seasons with non-league Blyth Spartans before Middlesbrough noticed his potential. He never quite became indispensable at Boro and was loaned to north-east neighbours Darlington in 1998. There he rapidly won over the fans. **'Lidds has the lot. Everything you need to be a hero at a club like ours. He's played through the pain, marshalled the defence and he always gives 120 per cent, if not more!'** Part of the fabric of the club, Craig is renowned for his last-gasp tackles when it looks as if the opposition must score.

Igor Stimac 1995–99

If you were guessing from scratch who would be a cult hero for Derby, you probably wouldn't immediately come up with a Croatian central defender – at least not if you were guessing before 1995. After that year, your plans would probably start to change quite radically. Igor Stimac joined for £1.5 million from Hajduk Split in October '95. Derby were near the foot of what was then Division One. He scored in his debut against Tranmere – the team lost 5–1, but then the charge started. Twenty games unbeaten and Derby surged up the table to win promotion to the Premiership. **'The man was a natural born leader. We could have got promoted with just one central defender once he arrived.'** High praise indeed for a player who used to serve in the Army. **'Unlike so many so-called hard men, Igor actually was, and you could see it in the opposition strikers' eyes. Not only that, he was married to an ex-Miss Yugoslavia ... lucky bugger!'**

Nominations Ted McMinn Dean Saunders Igor Stimac

Charlie Williams 1948–59

Now if you're looking for a cult hero who's seen a bit of life, look no further than Charlie Williams. Down the mines aged 14, Charlie played for Doncaster for 11 years from the late 1940s, but most of the public knew him as the black comedian with the Barnsley accent. He rose to television fame on the Seventies TV hit *The Comedians* and also had a stint hosting *The Golden Shot*. A truly incredible character, he lived through a difficult time for race relations. Many people had plenty to say on the subject of immigration, not least Enoch Powell. 'My mate Knockers ... ' Charlie would call him. The Doncaster fans particularly admired Charlie's continuing fondness for their club. 'I never saw him play, but when interviewed he always seemed so proud to have played for Rovers.' He *was* proud. And Charlie had one overriding philosophy: 'The pleasure is making people laugh – they can forget all about their electricity bills, their mortgages, their ailments. Laughter is the finest medicine in the world, and thank God I can still provide it.'

Graeme Sharp joined Dumbarton as a part-time player in 1978. His weekly wage was the princely sum of 25 pounds. It took about six months before the Glaswegian striker got a chance in the first team. When opportunity came his way he made absolutely sure he took it. The match was a local derby against Clydebank in the first division. Dumbarton ran out 3–1 winners with Graeme grabbing a couple of the goals for himself. From then his career snowballed. He scored 15 goals in the next 28 games, sending out a message to other clubs. **'Graeme was a quality striker for us. He signed straight from school and it was clear pretty quickly he wouldn't be with us for long. But all of us fans enjoyed his time and goals at the club.'** At the age of 20 Graeme's time with Dumbarton came to an end. Everton signed him up and by 1984 he'd scored a goal in

their 2–0 FA Cup win over Watford. The next season the Toffees won the League championship as well as the European Cup Winners' Cup and in 1986 Graeme went with Scotland to the Mexico World Cup. He later played for and managed Oldham Athletic.

Alan Gilzean 1959–64

Nominations Charlie Cooke **Alan Gilzean** Billy Steel

Alan Gilzean scored goals for fun, and it was this talent that made him a cult hero with the **D**undee fans. 'Gillie', as they all knew him, provisionally signed on at **D**ens **P**ark from **C**oupar **A**ngus **B**oys **C**lub in 1956, but it wasn't until 1959, after a couple of years in the Army, that he made his first-team debut. **A**lan soon became a regular and went on to score 165 goals in 185 league and cup games. In his final season at **D**undee he netted an incredible 52 goals. His prolific goalscoring ran parallel with **D**undee's glory years. In the 1961–62 season the club stunned **S**cottish football by breaking the dominance of the **O**ld **F**irm and taking the Division One title. **A**lan's goals were absolutely crucial. In fact he scored a brace in the game that confirmed the title victory. The next season he scored hat-tricks against **C**ologne and **S**porting **L**isbon and two against **A**nderlecht on the way to the semi-final of the European Cup. Eventually **A**lan left **D**undee to move to **T**ottenham **H**otspur for £72,500. By the time his career came to an end he had won 22 caps for **S**cotland as well as the **FA C**up and the **UEFA C**up with Spurs.

'Luggy' is what the fans affectionately nicknamed Paul Sturrock. **He played an important role in what was without doubt the greatest period in Dundee United's history.** As well as winning the Scottish championship in 1983, Paul was part of the side that reached the final of the UEFA Cup in 1987. He played in both legs of the final against Gothenberg which proved one step too far for his brave side. One of the main reasons they didn't quite have enough to take the trophy was that they played 67 competitive games that season. The side were mentally and physically shattered. Why particularly Paul Sturrock as their cult hero? Well, after joining as a 17-year-old he spent over a decade at Tannadice, first as a player and then as a coach. He then left to become manager at St Johnstone, but in the late Nineties he couldn't resist the pull of United, and he returned to take charge of his old club.

Istvan Kozma 1989–92

Dunfermline's all-time cult hero is also the man who won most international caps while playing at the club. 'The Hungarian Magician' played for his country 13 times while turning out for the Pars. Istvan Kozma says this period at the club was one of the happiest times of his life. In three years and just over 100 appearances he made an indelible impression on the Dunfermline faithful. He was brought to the club for a record fee – over half a million pounds – from Bordeaux. His most celebrated game was against St Mirren, in which he helped himself to an unforgettable hat-trick. '**He was the most skilful player I ever saw wearing the black and white of the Pars. Such a waste when Graeme Souness signed him for Liverpool and then he didn't get a game.**' Perhaps part of the frustration felt by fans towards Liverpool came from the terms of the deal that took Istvan away from Dunfermline. The club were suffering financially and ended up selling their jewel for a quarter of a million pounds less than they'd originally paid. Still, the fans who saw him say he was worth every penny.

Charlie Fleming 1947–55

If a top cult hero needs a top nickname, Charlie Fleming must have been great – he had two. 'Cannonball Charlie', an inside-right with a fearsome shot, was also known as 'Legs'. Charlie spent seven and a half years at Bayview, scoring 169 goals in only 241 appearances. Not the worst strike rate! It didn't take long for him to make the No. 8 shirt his own after joining the Fife from Blairhall Colliery in 1947. 'Legs' helped East Fife reach two cup finals in 1949–50. He was on the scoresheet in the League Cup final, helping his side to a 3–0 win over Dunfermline. Charlie didn't get a winner's medal afterwards, though. They weren't automatically presented in those days. **When East Fife offered the players a cash bonus or a medal, Charlie didn't think twice before taking the money, 'You can't eat a medal!' he said.** He played for Scotland and went on to sign for Sunderland, where again he scored like it was going out of fashion.

Gordon Russell 1984–2002

Gordon Russell must be one of the longest-serving members of a club never to win any silverware. For 18 years he shored up the defence of East Stirling, but could never win a promotion or a cup. In fact, the club has only won a league title once, and sadly that was in 1931–32. This fact never discouraged Gordon. He went on to play more games for the Firs Park club than anyone else in its history. A staggering 415 league appearances. 'We just loved Gordon for his commitment and honesty. Always happy and always giving more than 100 per cent every single season. The guy is a complete and utter legend.' Gordon, who was East Stirling's club captain, took over as caretaker boss when Brian Ross left. In February 2002 Gordon led his side to their first win over derby rivals Stirling Albion in over a decade. It was a thumping 3–0 win and cemented his cult status. Ironically, having not won a trophy in nearly two decades with East Stirling, Gordon moved to East Fife and won promotion in his very first season with the club!

Willie Grant 1959–67

Willie Grant was an amazing marksman at a time when Elgin City ruled the Highland League more firmly than at any other time in their history. While Willie was firing them in, his club won no fewer than six Highland League titles. They also captured a couple of Highland Cups too. The fans knew him as 'King' Willie. Perhaps an overstatement? Not when you realise he scored an incredible 348 goals – yes, 348 goals – in only 255 games for Elgin. If he could maintain that type of strike record, it would see him bag over 50 goals a season in today's Premiership! Nowadays if you ask a footballer his favourite way to relax, nine out of ten will tell you they are obsessed with golf. Willie was obviously well ahead of his time, as he subsequently moved on to be the starter at nearby **Garmouth & Kingston Golf Club.**

Neville Southall 1981–97

Neville Southall was a rock in goal during Everton's finest modern period in the Eighties. At that point he was arguably the best goalkeeper in the world. He helped Everton to win the League Championship in 1985 and 1987. He also won the FA Cup in 1984 and repeated the feat 11 years later. He was voted Football Writers Player of the Year in 1985, the same year the club won the European Cup Winners' Cup. By the time he moved on from Goodison Park, Big Nev had broken the club's all-time appearances record. He'd played between the sticks 751 times. Born in Llandudno, he also broke the Welsh national appearance record with 92 caps. Nev was never shy of giving his defenders a good rollicking – even when his side were winning comfortably. The fans loved how seriously he took his job: 'His exceptional ability between the sticks was only matched by his exceptional inability to smile!' The story goes that after Everton beat Manchester United in the FA Cup final, Nev didn't bother going to the celebration party, instead choosing to spend the night in front of the TV with his wife.

64

Kevin McAllister 1984–86, 1987–88, 1990–95 & 1997–01

Another cult hero, another intriguing nickname – 'Crunchie'. But no, Kevin McAllister has no particular fondness for honeycomb chocolate bars ... and the tag doesn't come from crunching tackles on the pitch either. As a youngster, Kevin played with a big kid who was known to all as 'Crunch'. Kevin somehow became known as 'Wee Crunchie' and eventually graduated to the full 'Crunchie' status that he holds today. Five thousand Falkirk fans turned out for Kevin's testimonial match against Hibs. It was a measure of the affection in which the fans hold him. They also voted him their player of the millennium. Kevin played for Chelsea in the Eighties but could never really resist returning to Falkirk. He had four spells there in all. The fans remember his trickery: **'Crunchie the genius with his dazzling runs and commitment ... that cheeky smile, and the moment he put Amoruso on his backside at Ibrox without even moving! A true sporting legend.'** In 1997 Kevin inspired Falkirk to beat Celtic in the Scottish Cup semi-final. They narrowly lost the final, but Kevin's goal against Huntley in an earlier round, where he beat eight players before scoring, was widely recognised as the goal of the season.

Nominations **Kevin McAllister** Simon Stainrod Chris Waddle

Stewart Kennedy 1980–90

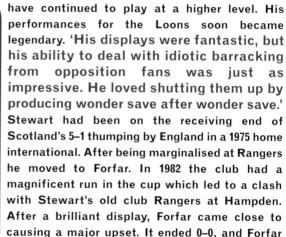

Stewart Kennedy is widely considered to be one of the greatest ever signings made by Forfar Athletic. The former Scotland goalie had previously been at Rangers, and many felt he could have continued to play at a higher level. His performances for the Loons soon became legendary. 'His displays were fantastic, but his ability to deal with idiotic barracking from opposition fans was just as impressive. He loved shutting them up by producing wonder save after wonder save.' Stewart had been on the receiving end of Scotland's 5–1 thumping by England in a 1975 home international. After being marginalised at Rangers he moved to Forfar. In 1982 the club had a magnificent run in the cup which led to a clash with Stewart's old club Rangers at Hampden. After a brilliant display, Forfar came close to causing a major upset. It ended 0–0, and Forfar were denied a hotly disputed penalty appeal in the last minute. A loss in the replay couldn't take the gloss off a wonderful achievement. In 1984, Stewart helped the Loons to win the second division title for the first time in the club's history.

Johnny Haynes 1952–70

The first ever £100 a week footballer, Johnny's greatest extravagance with his new-found 'fortune' was splashing out £3,000 on a brand-new S-type Jaguar in the Sixties. A stylish motor for the most stylish player ever seen at Craven Cottage. His trademark inch-perfect passing was executed on the old leather balls that were widely accepted to have weighed about two tons in the rain. He read the game so well, they said, that he could even anticipate what Jimmy Hill was about to do! Those skills and his enjoyment of the game made him the envy of home and visiting fans alike. Johnny was also known for making it clear to his team-mates what was expected of them on the pitch. A Fulham fan remembers being amused by 'his exaggerated theatrical histrionics when telling Tosh Chamberlain why he should have been on the end of a 40-yard pass five minutes earlier'. Johnny played 56 times for England and was part of the team that beat Scotland 9–3 in 1961.

Nominations Tosh Chamberlain Gordon Davies Johnny Haynes

Adrian Pennock 1996–2003

Variously described as a 'football genius' and a 'defender of no pace but astute in reading the game', **A**drian **P**ennock is widely recognised as the greatest comedian to have taken to the **P**riestfield stage. **'Always the first to give the sarcastic clap to the officials when they got a decision right (very rare at the Gills I assure you!), Adrian had plenty of other gags up his sleeve.'** This was typical of the responses we have received from many of the **G**illingham crowd. He scored a goal in his first home game, which is always a good start in winning over the crowd. **B**ut the defining moment in his popularity came in a crucial promotion clash with **W**igan in 2000. **I**n an attempt to clear a long ball, **A**drian in fact managed to slice it into the back of his own net. **G**illingham went on to win the game 2–1, but a new chant was born. **'O**wn goals, you only score own goals!' **W**henever it was sung from then on, **A**drian would always receive it with the same smile that he put on the faces of players and fans alike.

Paul 'Hags' O'Hagan 1987–94 & 1996–2000

Gretna is famous as the traditional marriage place for runaway couples. Fans of the club certainly had a love affair with Paul O'Hagan. 'Hags' was Gretna's do-or-die centre-back, as committed to the club as he was to every challenge on an opposition striker. 'The Rock' was around in the days when Gretna played in England before joining the Scottish divisions. He was key to the side's back-to-back championship wins starting in the 1990–91 season. Those titles lifted Gretna into the Northern Premier League. The club also had success in the Cumberland Senior Cup. In 1991 Gretna reached the FA Cup first round proper before losing 3–1 to Rochdale in front of a record home crowd of 2,307. Two years later at the same stage, they narrowly lost 3–2 to Bolton in a game played at Burden Park. **'A legend. He was Mr Gretna … You wouldn't even need to be at the ground to feel the shudder after some of his**

challenges.' Hags scored critical goals, including the opener in a 2–1 win against a full-strength Rangers side in January 1989. The game was staged to raise money for the Lockerbie disaster appeal. Hags was also voted Gretna's Players' Player of the Year three times.

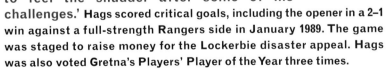

Nominations Les Armstrong Paul Lemming **Paul O'Hagan**

Gretna

Clive Mendonca 1992–97

Just as at Charlton, 'Super Clive' is how the Blundell Park faithful knew their most prolific striker of the Nineties. Eventually a string of bad injuries caught up with Clive, but at his best he was lethal. Alan Buckley paid £50,000 to bring him from Sheffield United, and it was an astute purchase. After a year-long injury in 1996, Clive made his comeback against Ipswich. Before you could blink he'd bagged a hat-trick, and he'd won the hearts of the fans all over again. Without the cruel injuries he would surely have been one of the great strikers of the time. Clive's best season was probably his last at Town. A 20-goal haul couldn't stop Grimsby being relegated, but the fans still adored him: '110 per cent every game and a great man too.' Later he famously scored a hat-trick in the thrilling play-off final that sent Charlton into the Premiership at the expense of Sunderland.

John McNaught 1982–86 & 1988

John McNaught died tragically young, but not before enriching the lives of so many Accies fans. A lovable rogue, John was a robust right-back who would run straight through his opponents. He also scored a remarkable number of times for Hamilton as a defender – 21 goals in 94 starts. In 1986 he helped Hamilton to the Scottish first division title. He was 21 years old and Chelsea stepped in to buy him for £90,000. Although he scored a couple of goals against David Seaman (then playing for QPR), John struggled to break into the first team regularly. Prone to off-field troubles, he was loaned by Chelsea to Partick Thistle. His stay at Firhill only lasted a matter of months before he returned to Hamilton in spring 1988. He helped the Accies win the first division title again, but the following season his spell in the Premier league was curtailed after just five games. **He was forced to retire from football as a result of a blood disorder which had caused him serious kidney problems.** A kidney transplant followed in the early 1990s, but in June 1997, having apparently returned to good health, he passed away suddenly and unexpectedly in his early thirties. John's nephew Tony Stevenson made his Hamilton first-team debut on 9 April 2005.

Joe Allon 1988–91 & 1995–98

At the end of his first stint at Hartlepool, Joe Allon's goals sent his side and grateful fans to promotion. A 3–1 victory over Northampton Town helped them to an automatic elevation and the season of 1990–91 had brought Joe a haul of 28 goals. The club had not seen scoring like it since Bill Robinson scored the same amount back in the Twenties. Things had not been so rosy when Joe first began at Hartlepool. The club looked destined to plummet. This is another reason why the fans took to Joe. 'He's a hero after helping us back from the brink of non-league football to win promotion in 1991.' His goals didn't go unnoticed and a £250,000 move to Chelsea followed. Opportunities at Stamford Bridge were limited, and Joe headed off to Brentford, Port Vale and, very briefly, Lincoln City before returning to his spiritual home for a few more seasons and quite a few more goals.

John Robertson 1980–98

Local rivalry plays a huge part in the fun of football. John Robertson's local club was Hibs, the sworn enemy of Edinburgh cousins Hearts. He could have had a career at Easter Road but was signed up astutely as a 16-year-old to play for Hearts instead. At five foot six, what he lacked in inches he made up for in goals. Many of them came against Hearts' deadly rivals. Between 1983 and 1998 there wasn't a year where he didn't score at least once against Hibs. By the time he hung up his boots, his personal derby total had reached 27 goals. After one encounter with Hibs, in which he grabbed a late equaliser, he commented, **'It's not over till the fat striker scores!' Of course the fans adored him – 'for his sheer brilliance on the pitch and most importantly for being the hammerer of Hibs'.** John scored in plenty of other games too. In fact he holds the club's all-time scoring record with 214 goals. He finished playing for Hearts on a high. He was on the bench and won his first medal for the club in the 1998 Scottish Cup final victory over Rangers. Not content with that, in 2004 he took over as manager of Hearts.

Heart of Midlothian

Nominations Drew Busby Jim Cruikshank John Robertson

Franck Sauzee 1999–2002

Franck Sauzee is probably the highest pedigree player ever to have played at Easter Road. Alex McLeish astutely signed the French international and European Cup winner for Hibs after Franck had a disagreement with his coach at Montpellier. Rapid Vienna and FC Basel were also sniffing around for a bargain, but Franck decided Hibernian was the club for him, and the fans can't thank him enough. **'He casually strolled through every game he played for us, rarely put a foot wrong and made many a player look foolish as he calmly flicked the ball over their head and carried the ball upfield. He brought a touch of class to Easter Road.'** Franck arrived in February 1999 and Hibs soon ran away with the first division title. In the top flight, Franck's ability stood him in good stead. By the time he finished playing, the club had reached the final of the Scottish Cup in 2001, where they lost out to Celtic, and they had also finished third in the Scottish Premier League. Earlier in his career Franck won the European Cup with Marseille, beating AC Milan 1–0 in the final in 1993. He also gained 39 caps for France, scoring nine times. In December 2001 he began an ill-fated 69 days as manager of Hibs, which sadly ended with the sack.

Iain Dunn 1992–97

You can't have a book of cult heroes without the odd supersub. Iain Dunn was such a player, often popping off the bench to change the course of a game. He even did it in the 1995 Division Two play-off final and set up Town's winner in the 2–1 victory over Bristol Rovers. His most distinguishing feature, however, was not his footballing talent but his lack of hair. One fan describes just how thatchless he was: 'He makes Zidane look like he has a Kevin Keegan style mullet!' On this basis a new song was created on the terraces, 'He's got no hair, but we don't care ... Iain Dunn, Iain Dunn!' The lack of follicles didn't affect his footballing brain, though. With 29 goals scored and many more set up, Iain Dunn's five years at Huddersfield left an unforgettable impression on the Yorkshire fans.

Huddersfield Town

Nominations **Iain Dunn** Steve Kindon Mark Lillis

Ken Wagstaff 1964–76

Ken Wagstaff joined Hull from Mansfield Town, whose supporters also chose him as their cult hero. It cost Hull £40,000 to bring Ken to Boothferry Park in November 1964. He was swiftly followed there by two other players, Ian Butler and Ken Houghton. Collectively they were tagged 'the Three Musketeers'. After an encouraging first season together, which just failed to bring promotion to Division Two, they went into the 1965–66 campaign determined to succeed. They didn't disappoint. In the FA Cup they knocked out opposition from higher divisions including Southampton and Nottingham Forest. In the quarter-finals a late equaliser by Ken took their tie with Chelsea to a replay before Hull were finally overcome. In the league they were irrepressible. A total of 62 goals from the Musketeers led to Hull winning the Division Three championship – at the time the greatest achievement in the club's history.

Jimmy Calder 1977–2002

Jimmy Calder almost qualifies for double cult hero status at the one club. His is truly a remarkable story. Born in Grantown-on-Spey, the Scot started his career as an outfield player. He played up front for Caley Thistle and was no mean striker when tragedy struck. A serious knee ligament injury left him unable to continue with the rigours of being a frontman. Rather than give up as a footballer, though, he decided to become a goalkeeper. At the age of 26, Caley Thistle gave him a chance between the sticks. That decision allowed Jimmy to be one of the major contributors to the greatest football headline of all time. In February 2000 Inverness beat mighty Celtic and Jimmy had a fantastic game. The *Sun* reported the match under the now famous headline **'Super Caley Go Ballistic, Celtic Are Atrocious.'** One fan sums up the eccentricities of Jimmy Calder the goalkeeper:

'Runs out of defence. Sitting on the crossbar and saving 50 per cent of the penalties taken against him. What a legend.' Jimmy made a comeback in the Highland League for Nairn County at the age of 44.

John Wark 1974–84, 1988–90 & 1991–97

John Wark has done just about everything. He's played at the back, in midfield and up front. He's won cups at home and in Europe. And, to cap it all, he's starred in a movie. All this he achieved while sporting his distinctive moustache. A Scot of great humour, John was spotted by Ipswich as a 15-year-old playing for Drumchapel Amateurs – the club that unearthed Archie Gemmill and Asa Hartford. It took a little while before, at the age of 17, John made his debut in an **FA Cup** sixth-round match against Leeds United in March 1975. The game was an epic. After three replays and John's commanding performance in central defence, Ipswich finally won the tie 3–2. The following year John was voted Ipswich's 'Young Player of the Year'. He moved into midfield and his scoring began in earnest. In league games he managed 135 goals with Ipswich in all. In 1978, Town reached the **FA Cup** final, playing Arsenal. In a shock result, Ipswich won the Cup 1–0. John hit the post twice. By 1981 the club, under the guidance of Bobby Robson, had also won the **UEFA Cup**. John scored 36 goals in the season

and was voted **PFA Player of the Year and European Young Player of the Year**. In the **UEFA Cup** run, his 14 goals broke the record set by **AC Milan's José Altafini in 1962**. John left Ipswich for Liverpool in 1984 for £450,000. With the Reds, he fulfilled his dream of winning the championship. But he returned to Portman Road in 1988, before again leaving, this time to Middlesbrough for a season. In 1991 he returned to East Anglia for the last time on a short contract. John had been thinking of retiring, but instead went on to play a further 188 games for the club! John played 29 times for Scotland, all under Jock Stein, and was his country's top scorer in the 1982 World Cup with two goals. **He managed to get involved in the cult film *Escape to Victory*, which was set in a prisoner of war camp and also featured Bobby Moore and Pele playing football in a cunning attempt to win their freedom. Unmissable.**

Paul Davies 1983–98

Nominations **Paul Davies** Delwyn Humphries Mike Marsh

Harriers fans picked the club's rough-and-tumble goalscorer as their all-time cult hero. Paul 'Ocker' Davies netted 295 goals in 656 games for Kidderminster – a true top-scoring ratio. Born in Kidderminster, Paul started off at Cardiff City before moving to Trowbridge Town. After leaving Trowbridge he went to the Dutch club SC Hercules of Enschede before coming back to the Harriers, at first on loan, then permanently for a fee of £1,500. Paul had the chance to turn professional with Wolves, but turned them down. Legend has it that the next day a young man called Steve Bull signed for the Black Country club. 'Ocker' is aptly described by one fan: 'Built like the proverbial outhouse, he was a target man in the traditional mould who served the Harriers for many years. Famous for his gap-toothed smile, he was less tough and ruthless, more rough and toothless!'

Ray Montgomerie 1988–99

'Big, strong, aggressive and tough. **N**ever in a million years was **R**ay a great footballer, but ask him to throw himself in front of a speeding train for the sake of the jersey and he would do it without thinking!' Ray Montgomerie was a true Scottish defender. He joined Killie from Dumbarton for £12,000. Shortly afterwards came the lowest point in his career, when he suffered the disappointment of relegation into the second division. But Ray was not a quitter. The club were promoted the next season, and by 1994 Kilmarnock had reached the promised land – the Scottish Premier League. This was a great achievement in itself, but more was to come. On 24 May 1997, Ray led Kilmarnock out for the final of the Scottish Cup against Falkirk. Killie had not won the cup for 68 years, but Ray did not plan on being denied. A typically gritty display, coupled with Paul Wright's winning goal, meant that captain Ray got to lift the cup and give the club its finest hour of recent times.

Billy Bremner 1959–76

Outside Elland Road there is a statue to Billy Bremner. It's a permanent reminder of the club's most influential player – a short but inspirational leader with a shock of red hair. By the time Billy joined Leeds, then languishing in Division Two, he had already been rejected by Chelsea and Arsenal for being too small. By the time he stopped playing, Leeds had reached the European Cup final, which was controversially lost to Bayern Munich, and Billy had also led them to the club's first two league titles as well as the League Cup, the FA Cup and two UEFA Cup (Fairs Cup) victories. He was voted Footballer of the Year in 1970 and won 54 caps for Scotland. Don Revie's side were hated by other clubs – for their gamesmanship, for pinching, for pulling other players' hair – but they had an unbreakable spirit, which Billy had helped create. If the little man could fight Dave Mackay, who would the rest of them be scared of? He was sent off in the 1974 Charity Shield with Kevin Keegan for a punch-up. Billy was a great tackler, a clever passer and scored more than most midfielders. In the mid Eighties he came back to manage Leeds. They narrowly lost an epic 1987 FA Cup semi-final 3–2 to eventual winners, Coventry. Billy passed away just before his 55th birthday, but will never be forgotten.

Steve Walsh 1986–2000

Steve Walsh was a central defender who feared no-one. Frequent sendings-off, plus broken noses, broken jaws ... sometimes it was his own body parts that suffered, sometimes those of others. He enjoyed classic running battles, none more memorable than his clashes with Wolves cult hero Steve Bull. **'The hardest footballer of the Eighties and Nineties by far. Sent off more times than Julian Dicks. Steve used to send Vinnie Jones home to look for his teddy bear!'** Steve also doubled up as a swashbuckling centre-forward and had a very creditable goalscoring record. Steve was made captain of Leicester for his incredible commitment and influence. Later he lost the captaincy, owing to continued disciplinary problems and suspensions, but eventually got it back. In 1994, following a terrible cruciate ligament injury, Steve returned for the tail end of the season. With Leicester losing 1–0 in the play-off final against Derby County, he came off the bench to score both Leicester goals in a 2–1 victory that sent them into the Premiership for the first time. In 1997 Steve held the League Cup aloft as Leicester beat Middlesbrough in the final after a replay. In 2000, his final season, Steve saw Leicester again win the League Cup against Tranmere. Perhaps fittingly, he was suspended for the final.

Nominations **Steve Claridge Steve Walsh** Frank Worthington

Leicester City

Peter Kitchen 1977–79 & 1982–84

Known as Cyrano, Peter Kitchen could smell a goal a mile off. During his time in East London, 'Kitch' scored some great goals, none more famous than the ones which helped his club's **FA C**up run to the semi-finals in 1978. Along the way Orient beat three top-flight clubs – Norwich, Middlesbrough and then Chelsea in a fifth-round replay at Stamford Bridge, in which Peter scored both Orient goals. Eventually they were overcome by Arsenal, who themselves were beaten by the underdogs, Ipswich Town, in the final. Peter also shares the record for most goals in one game for the O's. He bagged four in an old Division Two match against London rivals Millwall in April 1984. The fans remember his talents well. '**A first-class goalscorer, a lower-league Jimmy Greaves with his finishing but perhaps with better all-round awareness of his colleagues!**' Orient paid £45,000 for Peter when he first arrived from Doncaster Rovers. He scored over 100 goals in 250 appearances for Rovers.

Simon Yeo 2002–

One of the most contemporary cult hero choices by the fans. Simon Yeo's position in the hall of fame is cemented by his goalscoring exploits in the 2003 campaign which ended in the Division Three play-offs. He came off the bench to notch the goal that put City into one of those vital places. Then his cracking goals against Scunthorpe in the semi-final helped put them within one win of promotion. Sadly for Simon they were well beaten by a very strong Bournemouth side, but considering his club had been widely tipped for relegation to the Conference, Lincoln's progress was a minor miracle. Simon arrived at Sincil Bank with a poacher's reputation. He'd scored over 100 times in four seasons at Hyde United. He had also been a soldier and a postman in his career, and he stamped an immediate impression on the City fans when he first played in the league aged 28. **'Simon makes the crowd buzz throughout the game. When he shoots the crowd goes wild, and when he is brought on or off he always receives a massive standing ovation.'**

Nominations Gareth Ainsworth Mark Bailey **Simon Yeo**

Lincoln City

Robbie Fowler 1992–2001

'The Toxteth Terrier' wasted no time in making a name for himself on Merseyside. After scoring on his debut at Fulham in the Coca-Cola Cup he won the devotion of the Kop with five goals at Anfield in the return leg. He scored 12 times in his first 13 games and went on to net the Premiership's fastest hat-trick – in four minutes and 32 seconds against Arsenal. Perhaps his finest year was 1996, which saw Robbie's England call-up and 36 goals in the season. Liverpool fans loved the way Robbie wore his heart on his sleeve. **His 31 goals in the 1997 campaign came with a UEFA fine for displaying his 'Support the sacked Liverpool dockers' T-shirt after a goal.** In a game at Highbury he received a penalty for being brought down by David Seaman, but Robbie tried to convince the ref he hadn't been fouled. When he failed to do so, his weak penalty was saved, although Jason McAteer converted the rebound. Robbie got into hot water for 'sniffing' the touchline against Everton – a tongue-in-cheek celebration referring to fans' taunts of drug-taking. In 2001 he won UEFA Cup, FA Cup and League Cup medals, but it turned out to be his last full season at Anfield. Robbie fell out of favour with the Liverpool management, and much to the fans' dismay he was sold to Leeds for around £11 million.

Livingston

Marvin Andrews brought a little bit of Caribbean magic to Livingston when he arrived from Raith Rovers in 2000. The powerful defender was born in Sanguan, in Trinidad and Tobago, and went on to help Livi to the club's greatest achievements. He provided the spine for the club in his first full season as they rose into the Scottish Premier League. They then went on to qualify for the UEFA Cup. During the end of his time Livingston were in administration, but this didn't seem to affect Marvin's mood. 'He always had time for the fans. Played with a great big smile on his face. He was hard but clean.' When Marvin played for Trinidad and Tobago in the 2002 World Cup he gained the distinction of scoring the first goal in the competition. It came in a

qualifier against Netherlands Antilles. Marvin had a memorable final season with Livingston, when he was voted the club's player of the year. Livingston reached the semi-finals of the Scottish Cup, eventually losing to Celtic. In that same season Marvin won his first major medal, when he helped marshal the defence as Livi beat the favourites Hibernian 2–0 to win the Scottish League Cup final. The fans were sad to see Marvin leave, but didn't want to stand in his way when he left to play for Alex McLeish's Rangers in May 2004.

Nominations **Marvin Andrews** David Bingham David Fernandez

Mick Harford 1984–90 & 1991–92

Mick Harford used to terrify defenders. Tough as nails and a consistent goalscorer, he was a player that you wanted playing on your side. For the six years when he was considered to be at the top of his game and coveted by many of the top teams in the country and abroad, he played for Luton Town. The Hatters fans love the fact that he stayed put when many others took the cash. 'His loyalty speaks volumes, especially in the mid to late Eighties. Mick could have moved to a bigger club for the sake of his international career, but he didn't. He stayed with us at little old unfashionable Luton. Thanks Mick.' A very good first touch was another asset that helped him. Kenilworth Road had a plastic pitch and no-one worked out better how to play on it in front of goal. Once his playing career was over, Mick came back for spells coaching the Hatters. 'Even now Luton wins can be greeted by chants of "There's only one Mick Harford".'

John Askey 1984–2003

Known locally as 'Gentleman John', Askey played over 600 games for Macclesfield Town, scoring over 200 goals. Understandably the fans love him. **'As well as being a great attacker, he also played on the wing for years (when he had his speed!). John has always had the respect of the Macclesfield faithful, and when he was called upon to take charge at the club after David Moss left, our fans were right behind him even when things weren't going well.'** Twice John helped the Silkmen to win the Conference title. The second time, under Sammy McIlroy in 1997, they followed up by immediately winning promotion to Division Two – the club's greatest achievement. John's last league game made a fitting finale to his amazing career. John hadn't played in the first team for five months when he was brought on as a substitute against Rochdale in the last game of the 2002–03 season. When he came on, to rapturous applause, Macclesfield were trailing 2–1 with a quarter of an hour to go. By the end of the game he had reduced many in the crowd to tears, helping Macclesfield to a 3–2 victory and scoring a crucial goal himself with just two minutes left.

Macclesfield Town

Nominations John Askey Steve Burr Steve Wood

Colin Bell 1966–79

When Manchester City left their historic home of Maine Road to move into Manchester's Millennium Stadium, the club guaranteed that their favourite player would be remembered for generations to come. The Colin Bell Stand was built in tribute to a wonderfully elegant midfield player who could also run and run. Colin joined City in 1966 for £45,000 from Bury. In his debut game at Derby he got on the scoresheet. On this occasion it was not elegant – it was a deflection from Colin's back-side which provided goal number one. Ten games later, Colin had helped Man City win the title and promotion back into Division One. Shortly after he came to the club, Francis Lee was signed, to play alongside Mike Summerbee and Neil Young up front. Now City were really going places. In 1967–68 they won the Division One title after a memorable final game against Newcastle at St James's Park. Next was a 6–1 Charity Shield victory over West Bromwich Albion. But it was the 1969–70 season that provided a unique double. Domestically, Colin's side beat Leicester 1–0 in the **FA Cup** final. In the European Cup Winners' Cup final they overcame the Polish side **Gornik Zabrze** 2–1. Manchester City's manager Malcolm Allison nicknamed **Colin 'Nijinsky'**, after the famous racehorse with the legendary stamina, and the fans can't disagree with the description. **'A box to box player, one of the greatest athletes of all time and modest with it.'** The son of a miner, **Colin** could relate to the fans and he was never one to over-celebrate when he'd scored. He left that to others. **'Boy, did we "drink a drink a drink to Colin the king the king the king!" Legend.'** More honours followed, including a 2–1 extra-time League Cup final win against **West Brom** in 1970. **Colin** also made his mark internationally with 48 England caps – a record for a Manchester City player. Sadly, a knee injury forced **Colin** to quit the game prematurely at the age of 29. However, his tireless work for the community and charity fund-raising earned him an **MBE** in the 2005 New Year Honours List.

George Best 1963–74

George Best was one of the most remarkably gifted players ever to have lived. He was also football's original superstar and once proclaimed, 'I spent a lot of money on booze, birds and fast cars. The rest I just squandered.' He became an icon in the Sixties, and although many believe he didn't fulfil his true genius, he is still considered one of the greatest players ever to grace the planet. Belfast-born George made his debut for the Red Devils at the age of 17 in a 1–0 win over West Brom. He scored his first goal in his next match against Burnley. It was soon evident that 'Georgie' not only had sublime skill, but he also possessed amazing balance, wonderful vision and a sensational turn of pace. He was tough, too, considering his slight stature. George's first season saw Man Utd finish runners-up in the league. The following season, his first full campaign, saw United win the championship on goal difference from bitter rivals Leeds. Another Division One title came in 1967, and the following season brought an even greater prize. United reached the final of the European Cup, coming up against Eusebio's Benfica at Wembley stadium. The game went to extra time and, with United looking vulnerable, George scored a glorious solo goal to give United the lead. They went on to win the game 4–1 and become the first English team to win club football's biggest prize. George had scored 32 goals in 52 games that season and he was named 1968 Footballer of the Year and European Footballer of the Year. He was just 22 years old. George never won another medal. Although he continued to find the net regularly, the constant media exposure got the better of him. He partied hard and was seen as a playboy. In 1970 he scored six goals in an **FA C**up tie against **N**orthampton **T**own, but the overall picture was that he was drinking too much and becoming unreliable. **M**anchester **U**nited manager **T**ommy **D**ocherty's patience eventually ran out and he decided to get rid of George. His final game for United was on **N**ew Year's **D**ay 1974 at the age of 27. He later played for **L**os **A**ngeles **A**ztecs, **F**ulham and Hibernian, among others. In more recent times George has had a liver transplant as a result of his excessive drinking. However, along with many others, **P**ele still says that George was the greatest footballer ever.

Ken Wagstaff 1960–64

Plucked from the Mansfield Youth League, a 17-year-old Ken Wagstaff was chucked straight into the Stags side and scored both goals on his debut in a 2–1 win at Rochdale in 1960. A sign of things to come it surely was. By the 1962–63 season he'd forged a lethal partnership with Roy Chapman and bagged 40 goals as Mansfield were promoted from Division Four. The following season he continued stacking the goals up, and Hull City came knocking on the door. For £40,000, which was a lot of money in those days, Waggy headed off to Boothferry Park, where he also achieved cult hero status. But his time at Field Mill, with 105 goals in 196 games, left the Mansfield fans with many reasons to remember Ken fondly. 'The best player the Stags have ever had and will ever have,' says one. 'An entertainer who never disappointed, always smiled, never retaliated, just got up and on with his job. Waggy was so good, once he'd left us, I would go and see him play for Hull when Stags were not at home.' Many insist he was the best player never to play for England.

As one of Bernie Slaven's old team-mates puts it, 'The word legend doesn't do justice to Bernie!'. Born in Paisley in Scotland, he came to Middlesbrough in his mid twenties from Albion Rovers. At the time he was working as a part-time gardener! He soon fell in love with Boro nearly as much as the fans fell in love with him. Bernie scored 119 goals and after doing so enjoyed nothing more than throwing himself towards the jubilant crowd. The Wolfman, as he was known, decided to stand for the post of mayor of Middlesbrough. He could well have been elected, but in the end he decided to pull out because it would have meant giving up his jobs talking about football on radio and TV. He's been a legend on the airwaves. He promised that if Middlesbrough beat Manchester United he'd bare his backside in a local department store's window. Boro triumphed 3–2. Three thousand

spectators turned out to see Bernie keep his word. He was also 'arrested' for causing distress to Newcastle and Sunderland fans on his radio show. Three police officers later admitted it was a set-up by his old pals Malcolm Macdonald and Eric Gates.

Nominations Uwe Fuchs Juninho Bernie Slaven

Terry Hurlock 1987–90 & 1994

Not one of Millwall's nominations for cult hero status is a player who you would expect to see taking ballet lessons. Least of all Terry Hurlock. Terry grew up as a Millwall fan and a promising player who was spotted by West Ham. On his own admission, he knocked around pubs and clubs a bit too much in his youth. Eventually he got a second chance with Brentford, but it wasn't until he was 28 that he finally arrived at the Den. He was an instant success, helping to galvanise the club's midfield and winning over the supporters. **'A football fans' footballer, not like the prima donnas of today.'** Millwall were soon promoted to the top flight, and Terry was voted their player of the season. The rugged battler, who won three England 'B' caps, earned Millwall £375,000 when he signed for Rangers. He returned for a short spell in 1994, aged 35.

Alan Cork played for Wimbledon in the era before the club was moved and renamed, but it's clearly agreed by fans old and new that he is a player who deserves honouring. Alan joined Wimbledon in 1978, during their inaugural season in the old fourth division. His career then experienced just about everything imaginable. In 1979 the club went up again, and after a five-year yo-yo spell manager Dave Bassett led the team into the second division with two consecutive promotions. **Then, in 1986, Alan's goals helped Wimbledon achieve the remarkable feat of reaching the top flight of English football.** The club's first season with the big boys was a triumph. The Crazy Gang, as they were now known, clinched a top six finish. But the

best was still to come. Wimbledon reached the 1988 FA Cup Final. It was pure David and Goliath as they took on mighty Liverpool. Lawrie Sanchez's headed goal gave Wimbledon a 1–0 victory and a place in the history books. By the time Corky's fairytale career had finished, he had made 440 appearances, scored 145 goals, netted 29 goals in a season and four in one game – all of which remain club records.

Milton Keynes Dons
(formerly Wimbledon)

Nominations **Alan Cork** Vinnie Jones Dennis Wise

David Larter 1984 & 1987–98

So popular was **David Larter** as a goalie for **Montrose** that, after his career was ended by a back injury sustained in a cup tie, the supporters organised a testimonial match for him. It took months of recuperating to get **David** back on his feet, but the **Montrose** faithful felt they owed it to the player who faithfully guarded their sticks for over a decade and 426 league games. They even persuaded some players from rivals **Arbroath** (where **David** had also played at one time) to turn out in the strip of **Montrose**. This was some achievement as, much earlier in his career, **David** had a rather unfortunate altercation with **Arbroath** fans in a derby game. He was found guilty of flicking V-signs at them during a second division match at **Links Park**. **David** denied the charge, claiming he'd only put his arms in the air to celebrate a goal. **Arbroath Sheriff Court** disagreed and **David** was fined £300. As a player **David** appeared in all three of **Montrose**'s promotion-winning seasons. In 1991 and 1995 he was a regular, but he also played briefly as a triallist in **October 1984**, during the only other season in which **Montrose** had been promoted in the **Scottish League**.

Andy Ritchie is a cult hero with a special appeal for those who like to take things easy. Known as 'the Idle Idol', he was over six feet tall and played up front, and yet most who saw him claim that he couldn't jump, and that he rarely got his head on the ball. 'He was slow and lazy and always looked disinterested ... until the ball arrived at his feet, and then the magic would happen!' The fans were happy to forgive Andy seeming a tad overweight. **'I saw him volley a goal from the half-way line against Dundee United. He did what Pele only dreamt of!'** Andy joined Morton

from Celtic in 1976 in a swap deal for another player that netted Morton £10,000. Pretty good business by anybody's standards. In all he scored 133 goals in 246 games and was the top scorer in the Premier League for three consecutive years. Andy also won the Scottish Sports Writers' Player of the Year award. He will be most remembered for his magical free-kicks, wonderful passing vision and incredible goals.

Morton

Nominations Jimmy Cowan Allan McGraw Andy Ritchie

Bobby Graham 1973–77

Bobby Graham was born in Motherwell, but it wasn't until quite late in his career that he returned to capture the hearts of his hometown club. Bobby was an apprentice at Liverpool under Bill Shankly and signed professional forms at 17. He played alongside the likes of Roger Hunt and Ian St John. When St John later became manager of Motherwell, he brought in Bobby to provide guidance up front. 'We thought Bobby had come up north to see out the end of his career – he ended up in a famous double act with Willie Pettigrew. Bobby was one of the smartest players I ever saw.' The club's proudest moment came when they ended a remarkable post-war record sequence by Celtic. Under Jock Stein Celtic had reached seven successive Scottish Cup finals, winning five. In January 1976 Celtic lined up in the third round, looking to go on their first hat-trick of wins in the competition. Motherwell had other ideas. Celtic led through goals by Kenny Dalglish and Andy Lynch, but in a sensational comeback Motherwell levelled through goals by Bobby and Ian Taylor, before Willie Pettigrew grabbed the winner. Motherwell reached the semi-final against Rangers, which followed a similar pattern but with the roles reversed: Motherwell went 2–0 up, but were narrowly overcome 3–2.

Peter Beardsley 1983–87 & 1993–97

Newcastle United

Peter Beardsley is famous for his jinking runs, his ability to bamboozle defenders and some wonderful, wonderful goals. He was born a Geordie and he is loved by Geordies because of his attitude, effort and sheer talent. 'So clever. A first-class gentleman. He's respected, he's very approachable and has time for everyone in the community. A true ambassador for football.' Peter's first goals at St James's Park came in the form of a hat-trick in a 5–0 defeat over Manchester City. His 20 goals that first campaign helped Newcastle back into the top flight, where he continued to deliver the goods over the next three seasons. Peter was instrumental in helping England to the quarter-finals of the World Cup in 1986, and a year later Liverpool paid £1.9 million to take him to Merseyside, where the trophies soon mounted up. In 1993, aged 32, Peter made a dramatic return to Newcastle, now under Kevin Keegan. He struck up a prolific partnership with Andy Cole, and later with Les Ferdinand. In 1995–96 Newcastle looked certain to win the Premiership, after winning 19 of the first 25 games, but let it slip away. That was the closest Peter came to the title with Newcastle, but he continued to be idolised by the fans. 'He can't put a foot wrong. We even love his trademark "pudding bowl" haircut.'

Nominations Philippe Albert Faustino Asprilla Peter Beardsley

Andy Woodman 1995–99

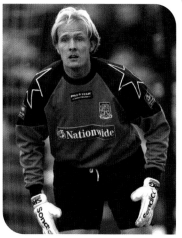

Andy **W**oodman has become famous mainly for being great friends with **G**areth **S**outhgate. **T**he pair wrote a fascinating book called *Woody and Nord: A Football Friendship*, about their relationship and contrasting careers since meeting at **C**rystal **P**alace. **S**outhgate has the nickname 'Nord', by the way, because he apparently sounds like **D**enis **N**orden! **H**owever, for fans of **N**orthampton, **W**oody is much more than just the mate of someone famous. **A**ndy kept sticks gamely for the **C**obblers and became more of a hero after his performances in two play-off finals. **T**he first came in 1997. **N**orthampton had never reached **W**embley in their 100-year history. **A**fter narrowly missing out on automatic promotion, the **C**obblers brushed **C**ardiff **C**ity aside in the semi-final to set up a promotion decider with **S**wansea **C**ity. **A**ndy put in a man-of-the-match performance, and John **F**rain's 90th-minute winner sealed promotion to the second division. **T**he following season **N**orthampton got to within one win of successive promotions, but despite **A**ndy saving a penalty in the play-off final against **G**rimsby, the **C**obblers just missed out, losing 1–0.

Bryan Gunn <space value="1986–98" />

Bryan Gunn was voted player of the year twice during his time at Norwich City and was integral to the club's most successful period. In all he played 477 games for the Canaries after joining from Aberdeen in 1986. **Bryan was always a brave keeper. He fought back from injuries ranging from a troublesome back problem to a broken ankle.** His courage was not confined to the pitch. His daughter Francesca suffered from leukaemia, and while she underwent chemotherapy, Bryan shaved his head to show his love and support. When, sadly, Francesca died from the disease, leukaemia research became Bryan's focus and he tirelessly used his profile to help with fundraising. Bryan, who also represented Scotland, was in goal when Norwich finished third in the Premiership in 1993. The following season they beat Bayern Munich during a fantastic UEFA Cup run which eventually ended with defeat by Inter Milan through goals by Dennis Bergkamp.

Nominations Robert Fleck **Bryan Gunn** Iwan Roberts

Stuart Pearce 1985–97

'Psycho' is surely one of the most fearsome sights any attacker has had to face in the past few decades. Thighs the circumference of an oak tree, a single-minded approach to win every ball, fifty-fifty or not, and a loyalty to his team that verged on the Kray-like. He had still been playing non-league football with Wealdstone into his twenties when he got a break at Coventry City in 1983. Two years later Stuart was brought to Forest by the legendary Brian Clough. Cloughie saw a leader in his tenacious left-back and by 1987 had made him captain of his neat, successful, passing side. In that same year, Stuart also started an England career that eventually brought him 78 caps. During that international journey Stuart had a penalty saved in the semi-final of Italia '90 against West Germany. It contributed to England's exit, so when, in the quarter-finals of Euro '96, England were involved in another shoot-out, the fans would have forgiven Stuart for leaving the spot-kicking to his team-mates. No chance. He took the ball and confidently fired home, exorcising all lingering demons. As he punched the air, roaring his celebration, no-one was left in any doubt about what it meant to Psycho. As well as being a tough tackler, Stuart was blessed with a thunderous shot. Many a 30-yard free-kick left keeper and wall stranded as the net bulged. In his final season at Forest, 1996–97, Stuart took over as player/manager, but was unable to prevent his team being relegated. It did, however, give him a taste for management, and in 2005 Stuart stepped up from coach to take charge at Manchester City following the resignation of Kevin Keegan. Who would bet against him one day taking over back at the City Ground?

Tommy Lawton 1947–52

Tommy Lawton created a sensation when he came to Meadow Lane in 1947. Notts County were in the depths of the third division, while Tommy was England's first choice centre-forward,

famous for his thunderbolt headers At the time the £20,000 transfer fee was a British record. His arrival from Chelsea instantly put 10,000 fans on the gate. A month later, on Boxing Day, 45,000 packed County's stadium. Another 10,000 were locked outside. Despite suffering from flat feet (he had to wear arch supports in his boots), Tommy became the youngest player to score a top-flight hat-trick when he netted all three against Spurs for Burnley in 1936, aged 17 years and four days. He also became the youngest scorer for England, at 19, in a 4–2 victory over Wales. In 1949–50 Tommy's goals helped Notts County to promotion to the second division. After 103 goals in 166 games for County he left to be player/manager of Brentford and then moved to Arsenal before returning to manage County. In his 20-year playing career he netted 231 goals in 390 league games, yet he was never once booked.

Andy Ritchie 1987–95

'He's got no hair but we don't care!' has been sung by a few football crowds in its time, but probably never with such tenderness as when directed at Andy Ritchie from the Chaddy End of Boundary Park. 'Stitch', as Ritchie is known by the Oldham faithful, played for some massive teams in his time. But forget the Uniteds of Leeds and Manchester – it's Oldham where the fans have voted him number one. He joined in 1987, immediately after having helped second division Leeds reach the semi-final of the FA Cup. They unluckily lost to eventual winners Coventry City. In his first Latics season he missed eight matches due to a hamstring injury but still scored 19 league goals. By the time he left the club as a player he'd scored 105 goals in 250 games, and he'd been with Athletic through some of their most successful periods in modern times. 'He drew gasps of disbelief when he conjured up some sublime magic. We had no-one to replace him when he left, that's why we dropped down the divisions.' With the fans' approval Andy returned for a period as Oldham's boss in 1998.

Nominations Rick Holden Roger Palmer **Andy Ritchie**

107

John Aldridge 1984–87

John Aldridge, or 'Aldo,' joined **O**xford **U**nited from **N**ewport County in 1984 for £78,000. Three years later, for a fee nearly ten times that amount, he moved on to play alongside **I**an **R**ush at **L**iverpool. The reason for the price hike was pretty clear. **S**oon after he joined, he became part of the **O**xford side that took the third division title. **W**hen the **I**rish international **B**illy **H**amilton arrived, **J**ohn really started finding the back of the net. **He became the first Division Two player for two decades to score 30 league goals in a season.** It was this prolific goalscoring that guided **O**xford into the top flight. **T**he club struggled in **D**ivision **O**ne, but **A**ldo didn't. **A**t a time when **R**ush and **L**ineker were at the top of their game, **J**ohn finished the season as the third highest scorer in the division. **H**e bagged 31 goals in all competitions. **I**n the **L**eague **C**up he scored in the semi-final first leg at **V**illa before helping his side thrash **QPR** 3–0 to win the trophy. **A** few weeks later he scored as **U**nited beat **A**rsenal 3–0 and ensured their survival in the top division. **W**hile at the **M**anor **G**round, as well as scoring 90 goals in 141 games, **J**ohn also won the first of his 69 caps for the **R**epublic of **I**reland.

Denis McQuade 1970–78

Denis McQuade was an original. A six-foot, two-inch winger who could dazzle or disappoint at any time. **'Eccentric hero of ours.**

Denis was the type who could beat five defenders with a mazy dribble and then miss the open goal!' He could play on either wing and was always worth paying to see. 'Exhilarating. "Daft" Denis's feet operated independently of his brain!' Those feet, however, played a key role in Thistle's most memorable victory. Denis was a 19-year-old student at Glasgow University when Thistle set out on their Scottish League Cup journey. In the semi-final, his two goals finished off Falkirk, which meant a place in the final – against the mighty Celtic. So, in October 1971, the final began and by half-time the score was 4–0 ... to Partick Thistle! Denis had scored, along with Alex Rae, Bobby Lawrie and Jimmy Bone. Celtic attacked fiercely, Kenny

Dalglish got a goal back and Thistle were under the cosh for almost the entire second half. But they hung on for a famous victory. Denis was later a member of the Thistle side that won the first division championship – and promotion into the Scottish Premier Division.

Ken Charlery 1991–92, 1993–95 & 1996–97

Every time **Ken Charlery** left **Peterborough United**, he just couldn't resist coming back again. He had three separate spells as the darling of the **Posh** fans. Perhaps it was the success of the first of these that helped to secure him the position of the club's all-time cult hero. The year was 1992. The event was Peterborough's first appearance at **Wembley**, when going for promotion in the **Division Three** play-off final. They faced **Stockport**, and **Ken** had already scored one vital goal for **Posh** when late on he grabbed the winner in a 2–1 victory. It made history for the club and a hero of **Ken**. '**I** remember watching this guy when he first signed for us and wondering if he would ever make it in football. Years later he was still banging the goals in for **Posh** (including a couple we'll never forget at Wembley) and we loved him so much we bought him back about 99 times!'

Peterhead

John Sievwright had a phenomenal career at Peterhead. He commanded their rearguard from central defence for a full twenty years and he won the admiration of the fans. 'One of the true gentlemen of Scottish football, schoolteacher John was a rock at the heart of the Blue Toon defence.' His father, John 'Jock' Sievwright, had also played in defence for Peterhead. Our cult hero, John 'Sivvy' Sievwright, was playing at a couple of landmark moments for the club. In 1987 Peterhead had their greatest ever run in the Scottish Cup. After knocking out East Stirlingshire, Rothes and Clyde, Peterhead were only thwarted in the fourth round by Raith Rovers. It was an epic encounter that was only settled after a third replay! But perhaps the greatest moment in John's career came after he'd been at the club for 16 years. In 1989 Peterhead took the Highland League championship for the first time since 1950.

Nominations Charlie Duncan **John Sievwright** Brian Third

Tommy Tynan 1983–85, 1986–90

Tommy Tynan is **Plymouth Argyle's** leading post-war **goalscorer** and was recognised as the most consistent lower-league poacher during his time in the **West Country. A S**couser by birth, **Tommy's** career got off to an unusual start. The Liverpool Echo ran a 'search for a star' competition, with the winners getting trials at **Anfield. Tommy** took his chance and scored five goals in the trial to sign as an apprentice at Liverpool. He couldn't break through and, after a successful stint with **Newport County, Tommy** signed for **Plymouth** in **1983** for **£55,000. He** had a slow start with the third division strugglers but finished his first season with **16** goals. These included three in the **FA C**up as the Pilgrims had a fantastic run to the semi-finals, eventually losing 1–0 to **Watford. N**ext season was even better, bringing 32 goals. Then came a massive shock for the **Plymouth** fans. **Tommy's** family wanted to move back up north, and he left for **Rotherham. However, at the end of the 1985–86** season **Tommy** returned on loan, and his ten goals in the last nine games sealed **Argyle's** promotion to Division Two. **By** the time he left **Plymouth, Tommy** had scored 126 goals in 261 league appearances.

Alan Knight

No goalkeeper has ever played more games for a single club than **A**lan **K**night. **H**e beat the record of the great **C**helsea keeper **P**eter 'the **C**at' **B**onetti in the mid **N**ineties and went on to make a total of 801 appearances for **P**ompey in all competitions. **I**n a career spanning four decades with the club, **A**lan saw it all. **W**hen he made his debut against **R**otherham, keeping a clean sheet, **P**ortsmouth were in the old fourth division. **I**n his time the club progressed up through the divisions to the top flight. '**H**e was a consummate professional, a superb shot-stopper and a loyal servant to the club. **A** rare breed.' **A**lan so nearly realised his dream of playing in the **FA C**up final. **I**n 1992 **P**ortsmouth played **L**iverpool in the semi-final of the competition. **T**he game went to penalties and, agonisingly, **P**ompey became the first club to miss out on **W**embley via a shoot-out. **A**lan went on to become the club's goalie coach, and on one occasion, owing to injuries, was forced back on to the bench for a match at the age of 42! **H**e was awarded a well-deserved **MBE** in recognition of his loyal service to **P**ortsmouth and the game.

Nominations Alan Biley **Alan Knight** Paul Walsh

Neil Aspin 1989–99

With more than 400 appearances over ten years at the Vale, Neil Aspin was the definition of effort, endeavour and reliability. The super-solid defender netted on a few occasions too, as the fans well remember. **'Three goals in a decade, each celebrated as though we'd won the World Cup!'** Amazingly, before Neil joined Port Vale, he had already had a significant seven-year career with Leeds United, including an FA Cup semi-final appearance that was so unexpected he was forced to postpone his wedding. The truth was that Neil was not the most naturally gifted defender the world had ever seen, but what he was not provided with by nature, he made up for by pure determination. **'Played for us until he could barely walk – the man never gave less than his all, often in dire circumstances. I remember him insisting on marking the giant Kevin Francis despite a ridiculous height difference!'** His total baldness was also seen as a cult virtue.

Tom Finney 1946–60

Legend has it that, on his debut, **Tom Finney's** trainer said to him, 'Don't worry, son, we're not expecting too much from you.' The next decade and a half must have been a pleasant surprise. A part-time plumber for most of his playing days, a gentleman on the pitch and now the club's president, **Tom** was a versatile outside-right. A prolific goalscorer, he ran defenders ragged and made many more goals than he scored. 'He played in every position across the forward line for club and for country. Tom was always compared to Stanley Matthews, but there was no comparison as Stan only played in the one position.' **Tom** scored 210 goals in 473 games for **Preston**, and 30 for **England** in 76 internationals. **Tom** remained in **Preston** throughout his career, even though their only silverware was the second division title in 1951. Italian club **Palermo** failed to tempt him away with an offer – huge for the time – of £10,000, a villa and a car. **Tom** was crowned **Footballer** of the Year in 1954 and 1957. **Preston** finished second in **Division One** in 1953 and 1958 and lost 3–2 to **West Brom** in the 1954 **FA Cup** final. In 1996 **Preston** unveiled the **Tom Finney Stand**, which became the **Sir Tom Finney Stand** in 1998 when he was knighted.

Preston North End

Nominations Alex Bruce **Tom Finney** Brian Mooney

Tommy Bryce 1993–98 & 1999

Tommy Bryce has always been adored by the Queen of the South fans. And he goes down in history for one achievement above all others. It's also probably the reason he secured cult hero status over the other nominees. It came about on a dull wet December day in 1993. A crowd of 482 were present as Queen of the South took on Arbroath. The score was 0–0 and there wasn't much to talk about. One hundred and ten seconds later, Queen of the South were three goals up, and Tommy Bryce had entered the Guinness Book of Records as the fastest scorer of a hat-trick in footballing history. Not long after that, Tommy scored another

hat-trick in under three minutes. The fans think he could have bettered his original record: 'Tommy's second hat-trick would have been quicker, but he over-celebrated his second goal with the clock still ticking!'

Brian McPhee 1993–96

The Spiders legend shares the same birthday as his hero Pele, and at Queen's Park Brian is just as popular as the great man. Brian was a late starter in the Scottish leagues. He'd reached his mid-twenties before he got his break at Queen's Park. Supposedly he was unearthed by a club director who drank in the pub where Brian worked. His pace and finishing soon caught the eye of bigger clubs, but not before he had won the hearts of the Hampden faithful. The fans' favourite song of the time was 'Ooo Eee Brian McPhee, I said Ooo Eee Brian McPhee!' But Brian wasn't content just to have songs sung about him. After moving to Hamilton Academicals Brian decided he had a decent voice and took part in a *Fame Academy* spoof on Tam Cowan's *Offside* show. **He chose to perform UB40's hit 'Kingston Town'. Perhaps Brian's vocals don't quite match his speed over five yards, but he's loved all the same.**

Queen's Park

Nominations Mickey Hendry Peter McNamee Brian McPhee

Nominations **Stan Bowles** Les Ferdinand Rodney Marsh

Stan Bowles 1972–79

What do you do? You're a keen gambler. You're in desperate need of some cash and – just like London buses – two famous football sponsors offer big bucks if you'll wear their boots in the match on Saturday. The Stan Bowles solution was simple. Wear odd boots! Another time, in order to make some money, he announced his retirement from the game in one of the papers. The next day he announced he was making a comeback. **'In the greatest QPR team of all time, Stan was the maestro. His game on the pitch was matched by his antics off it ... Even today, thirty years on, he receives hero worship from young and old alike at Loftus Road.'** Stan's football was a joy, and in 1976 he helped his club to within a whisker of winning the league championship. **QPR** were pipped by Liverpool, but qualified for the **UEFA C**up. Considering his huge talent, Stan didn't play nearly enough for England. He once walked out on an England squad training session, and was found later at the White City dog track.

Gordon Dalziel's nose is the most popular nose in Kirkcaldy. Although he still insists it was with his head that he scored the goal that helped bring Raith Rovers' finest hour, most fans prefer to perpetuate the nasal legend. People still stop him in the street to stroke it. It all dates back to 1994, when Raith reached the final of the Scottish League Cup. Their opponents were the mighty Celtic. With the clock ticking down, Raith were trailing 2–1. But 'Daz' had not become a Stark's Park legend without being able to sniff out a goal chance. The club's record scorer got something on the ball, putting it in the net and taking the final to extra

time. It went to penalties, and Raith's keeper saved Celtic skipper Paul McStay's kick to provide a memorable victory. Gordon moved into management and after six years at Ayr returned to take charge at Raith. **'No other player has had the impact on Raith that he has. Goalscoring machine, jokesmith and all-time wee devil!'**

Ally McCoist 1983–98

When you see the funny bloke on **BBC1**'s *A Question of Sport* bantering with **Sue Barker**, it's easy to forget that **Ally McCoist** also has an unparalleled scoring record for **Rangers**. Over 15 wonderful years with the club he managed to notch up 355 goals in 581 games. He also fired in 28 hat-tricks – twice managing to score five hat-tricks in a single season! 'He was the most discreet poacher in the history of **S**cottish football! **P**ulled **R**angers through many bad games and was always guaranteed to score in those famous trips to **C**eltic **P**ark. He was also known for his practical jokes ... especially at the expense of **C**eltic players!' **A**lly began his career at **S**t **J**ohnstone and then moved to **S**underland, but at that point no-one could have foreseen the career that would follow. A fee of £185,000 took him to **I**brox, and once he'd settled in, the goals began to come. In 1984 he won over the fans, scoring a hat-trick against Celtic in the League Cup final. Ally's highest haul of league goals in a season was 34. He managed that three times, in 1986–87, 1991–92 and 1992–93. On the second of those occasions he became the first Scottish player to win the European Golden Boot – an award he was also given the following season. In October 1992 he scored four goals in a match against Falkirk. But it was in Old Firm games where Ally particularly thrived. He scored against Celtic on no less than 27 occasions – more than any other player in the last 100 years. From 1989, Rangers won nine Scottish league titles in a row. Ally was one of only three players who featured in every year of that amazing run. He won ten titles in all. Ally also scored 19 goals in 61 games for Scotland and played in the 1990 World Cup in Italy. In 1994 he received an MBE. In 1998, Ally left Rangers for Kilmarnock, where he played for three years before retiring to follow his path in the media.

Robin Friday 1974–76

Nominations **Robin Friday** Michael Gilkes Phil Parkinson

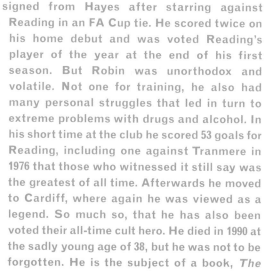

Robin Friday is the footballing definition of rock 'n' roll. The most charismatic player ever to wear a Royals shirt, he was also the most tragic. Robin was signed from Hayes after starring against Reading in an FA Cup tie. He scored twice on his home debut and was voted Reading's player of the year at the end of his first season. But Robin was unorthodox and volatile. Not one for training, he also had many personal struggles that led in turn to extreme problems with drugs and alcohol. In his short time at the club he scored 53 goals for Reading, including one against Tranmere in 1976 that those who witnessed it still say was the greatest of all time. Afterwards he moved to Cardiff, where again he was viewed as a legend. So much so, that he has also been voted their all-time cult hero. He died in 1990 at the sadly young age of 38, but he was not to be forgotten. He is the subject of a book, *The Greatest Footballer You Never Saw*, written by Paolo Hewitt and Oasis bassist Paul McGuigan.

Reg Jenkins 1964–72

Most of the fans at Rochdale consider Reg Jenkins to be the club's greatest ever signing. Reg joined from Torquay in 1964 and hit the ground running with two goals in his first game at Spotland. In that campaign he helped himself to 25 goals, and over the next eight seasons he never stopped scoring. He wasn't particularly quick; he wasn't unbelievably skilful, but what he could do was shoot with both feet – and what a shot it was. Reg was known for spectacular thunderbolts flying in from all distances and angles. He passed Bert Whitehurst's club goalscoring record and eventually ended up with 141 goals in 359 appearances. He'd celebrate his goals with merely a raised hand. 'Legs like tree trunks, he'd use his giant frame to give himself the half a yard he needed to get his shot in.' On one occasion he even gave the Rochdale rugby side a few problems. There was a special half football, half rugby game, and the ref gave a few rugby penalties which Reg happily converted from near and far.

Billy Ferries 1982–99

Nominations John Buchanan **Billy Ferries** Jim Hosie

When the final whistle went at Brechin City on the first Saturday of April 1999, Billy Ferries broke down in tears. Ross County had clinched the third division title and Billy had completed a career journey which had begun with County as a non-league side. In his early days the shower at the club had to be turned on with a spanner. Perhaps it was these technical skills that later encouraged him to set up his kitchen fitting business. Billy was a winger and spent well over a decade tormenting teams outside the Scottish League. In the early Nineties he helped the Victoria Park club to back-to-back Highland League title triumphs. **'Billy was a box to box winger who could play on both sides of the park. He dazzled the crowds with mazy runs and not only set up but scored many spectacular goals.'** Eventually Billy finished off with Brora Rangers. He suffered a heart scare during a game, but considered the Highland League the best in Scotland because of the atmosphere and the 'wee refreshment' after games.

Ronnie Moore 1980–83

Ronnie Moore is worshipped by Millers fans for two reasons in particular. It all started in the early Eighties, when Ronnie played up front for Rotherham. 'He was a fantastic centre-forward who always had a trick up his sleeve to get a goal when it mattered.' His goals went a long way in helping Rotherham becoming Division Three champions in 1980–81. More than a decade and a half later, Ronnie took the reins as manager of a club in crisis. They'd been relegated into the third division and had almost no money. Just the sort of challenge Ronnie loves. With a mixture of good humour and skilful man-management he took Rotherham to successive promotions in 2000 and 2001, to put the club in the unlikely position of being just one league below the Premiership. 'He's simply God! A fantastic scorer for us in the Eighties and since an immortal manager. Could you ask Mark Lawrenson to stop singing his praises on *Football Focus*? Otherwise someone will hear how good he is!' Too late! Ronnie's now boss at Oldham.

Nominations Alan Lee **Ronnie Moore** Bobby Williamson

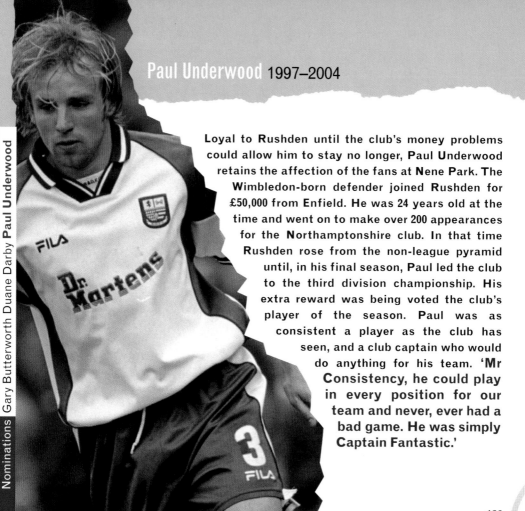

Nominations Gary Butterworth Duane Darby **Paul Underwood**

Paul Underwood 1997–2004

Loyal to Rushden until the club's money problems could allow him to stay no longer, Paul Underwood retains the affection of the fans at Nene Park. The Wimbledon-born defender joined Rushden for £50,000 from Enfield. He was 24 years old at the time and went on to make over 200 appearances for the Northamptonshire club. In that time Rushden rose from the non-league pyramid until, in his final season, Paul led the club to the third division championship. His extra reward was being voted the club's player of the season. Paul was as consistent a player as the club has seen, and a club captain who would do anything for his team. '**Mr Consistency, he could play in every position for our team and never, ever had a bad game. He was simply Captain Fantastic.**'

'Not the quickest!' is one way in which St Johnstone fans describe their beloved striker. Roddy was legendary for his lack of pace, but his first touch, close control and finishing were second to none. His team-mates worked to get him the ball, then Roddy would do the rest. In both his spells at the club, Roddy managed to help bring promotion to McDiarmid Park. In 1989–90 St Johnstone were battling it out for the title with Old Airdrieonians. The crunch game towards the end of the season was at St Johnstone on a scorching hot day. Roddy's team fell behind, but he inspired them to a 3–1 victory – on the way scoring with a good header. The win effectively ensured the Scottish first division title. Roddy never exactly lived the life of an athlete – mixing freely with the fans. He'd joined the club as a trained stonemason and never had any pretensions. Tall, but by no means lean, Roddy

left for Dunfermline in 1992, but four years later returned. Under manager Paul Sturrock, Roddy again scored the goals that helped St Johnstone to win the first division championship in 1996–97.

Mark Yardley 1995–2003

Mark Yardley is a striker who can't resist making an immediate impact at his clubs. When he returned to Cowdenbeath, the team he'd played for as a kid, he scored four goals on his debut. So when he joined St Mirren, at the age of 26, he knew he needed to do something pretty spectacular to trump that. On the pitch for the first time he pondered what this could be for less than 60 seconds before he found the back of the net – in his first minute with his new club. Over the next six and a half years his scoring touch never left him, and he was a massive favourite with Saints fans both for this and for his committed style of play. Once, when St Mirren had their keeper sent off and were 3–0 down, 'Yards' appeared for the second half wearing the goalie jersey. Forty-five minutes later he'd made some terrific saves and his side went down fighting 4–2. His final goal for St Mirren was one of his greatest. Mark beat three defenders and unleashed an unstoppable shot to give Saints a 3–2 League Cup victory over rivals Morton.

Very early on after arriving from Spain, Alex Calvo-Garcia took Scunthorpe to his heart. One fan remembers a radio interview in which Alex was asked how Scunny compared to his home town: **'Ahhh ... the laydeeezz of Scunthorpe ... veeery nice, I like a lot!'** Starting out as a striker, Alex soon converted into a battling, attack-minded midfielder. In 1998 the club just missed out on the Division Three play-offs by one point, but the following season they were not to be denied a chance at promotion. Scunthorpe reached the play-off final against Leyton Orient at Wembley. Alex brought his family over to watch. His mum didn't enjoy flying so it was the first time they'd seen him play in four years. He didn't disappoint, and after five minutes Alex scored the goal that secured his club promotion and him a place as a cult hero. His well-earned testimonial at the club featured stars including Mendieta, Campo and Jordi Cruyff.

Tony Currie 1968–76

Tony Currie was an entertainer. Wonderful skills, graceful movement and a handful in midfield for every team that came up against him. 'Tony could do things that even now I think cheated science! He was a velvet magician who could bamboozle every defender in the land.' In a

famous Seventies commentary line by John Motson, one particular Tony goal is simply described as 'a quality goal by a quality player'. Tony was certainly quality. He arrived at Bramall Lane in 1968 from Watford for a bargain £26,500. For the next eight seasons he had the Blades crowd on the edge of their seats, waiting for his next bit of inspiration. 'He was simply awesome in midfield. Classy, with a great shot from distance. Tony could land a 60-yard pass on a sixpence.' It didn't take him long to help Sheffield United into the top flight. His form in the 1970–71 Division Two campaign helped United to the

runners-up spot – and it gave Tony a chance to show off his immense ability against the big boys in Division One. Internationally, Tony won 17 caps for England. If the national side had been able to support more flair in that period, he would surely have played many more times. In 1976, after more than 300 appearances for the Blades, Tony moved to rivals Leeds for £250,000. After finishing playing, Tony's contribution to football did not end. He has spent many years organising football projects in the local community for Sheffield United. His contribution to Yorkshire football has been fantastic.

Terry Curran 1979–82

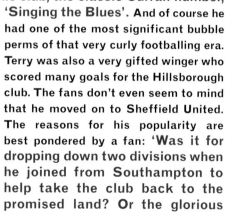

There are countless reasons why **Terry Curran** is so popular with **Owls** fans. He scored an unforgettable goal against deadly rivals **Sheffield United** in a **Boxing Day** derby match in 1980 at **Bramall Lane**. Four-nil victories in that fixture stick in the mind. **Terry** also recorded a track in honour of his club, the classic **Curran** number, **'Singing the Blues'**. And of course he had one of the most significant bubble perms of that very curly footballing era. **Terry** was also a very gifted winger who scored many goals for the **Hillsborough** club. The fans don't even seem to mind that he moved on to **Sheffield United**. The reasons for his popularity are best pondered by a fan: **'Was it for dropping down two divisions when he joined from Southampton to help take the club back to the promised land? Or the glorious** goal against the **Blades**? Would he have been the same player without that hair and 'tache? Whatever, we love him!'

Dean Spink is a truly multi-talented fellow. Just ask the fans of Shrewsbury Town. In over 300 appearances at Gay Meadow he played up front getting the goals, and he also played at the back helping to keep clean sheets. Another talent was being a half-decent looky-likey for the Scottish rock star Rod Stewart. The voice apparently was not quite in the same league. **He was the darling of the crowd and probably had his best season in 1993–94.** His 22 goals included a memorable hat-trick against Wigan, and they contributed to Shrewsbury winning the third division title. Dean had started off with non-league Halesowen and worked as a window cleaner to help pay the bills. Aston Villa took a £30,000 gamble on him, but he didn't get much opportunity, and so Asa Hartford spent £75,000 bringing him to Gay Meadow. One last talent should be mentioned. After retiring he went on to become Shrewsbury's senior physiotherapist.

Nominations Steve Anthrobus Austin Berkeley Dean Spink

Shrewsbury Town

Matt Le Tissier 1986–2002

Matt Le Tissier is thought of by many as the perfect bloke. He grew up on the tranquil channel island of Guernsey. Then he moved to Southampton, the nearest club to him geographically on the English mainland. He stayed there for his entire career, in spite of lucrative offers from bigger clubs, and helped them to stay in the Premiership, regularly cheating relegation by performing David and Goliath acts. He scored some of the most memorable goals of his era, while carrying a figure that would not have looked out of place in a darts championship. On top of all that he managed to date a soap star and be referred to by Saints fans as 'Le God'. He was the master penalty-taker, scoring 49 times out of 50. He managed 209 goals in a career that spanned 16 years. Matt was also the scourge of Manchester United. In particular the 6–3 thrashing of the Reds in 1996 springs to mind. Le Tiss bossed the show and provided the game's highlight when he glided past Brian McClair and Gary Pallister and then with a sublime right-foot chip left Peter Schmeichel stranded. Even at the end of his career Matt was able to provide something extra special. In the last game ever played at the Dell, Matt typified the romance he'd brought to the club. The opponents were Arsenal. Matt was half fit at most. The score was 2–2 when, with 20 minutes to go, Matt was brought on as a sub. Everyone surely thought this was a token gesture in gratitude for all his wonderful service. **Then in the**

final minute **Le Tiss** got the ball with his back to goal. **A** swivel and shot later he left the fans with the most magical moment they could ever know. **Le God** indeed.

Chris Powell 1990–96

Chris Powell was Southend United's greatest ever left-back. He also played a big part in the most successful period in the Shrimpers' history. Born in Lambeth, he walked into the award of Southend cult hero. What seems to have given him the edge over some very stiff competition is his likeable persona. He could charm anybody with his pleasant manner. 'Could quite easily be considered one of the nicest men in football, a true gent. The fans had seen us lose at Stoke and we knew Derby were ready to poach him, so we started singing "Don't go, Chrissy, don't go", to which he turned round and gave us one of his broad smiles, waving as he left the pitch – the next week he was gone!' Southend were £800,000 better off for selling Chris. Not bad as he'd come on a free transfer from Crystal Palace. Eventually Sven was won over by his performances for Charlton and called the ex-Roots Hall man up to play for England.

Graeme Armstrong 1992–2000

Graeme Armstrong holds the Scottish record for outfield league appearances. Over a quarter of a century, playing for Stirling Albion, Berwick Rangers, Meadowbank Thistle, Stenhousemuir and Alloa, he ran up 909 appearances in the league and 1,053 games overall. He played his 1,000th competitive game at Ibrox against Rangers and was afforded a guard of honour in recognition of his remarkable achievement. He was still playing in the Scottish first division at the age of 43! Graeme helped guide Stenhousemuir to their first ever trophy in 1995. The Warriors had not reached a final in their 111-year history until they came up against the much fancied Dundee United in the Scottish League Challenge Cup. After holding United goalless in normal and extra time, the Warriors won the penalty shoot-out 5–4 to humiliate the Tannadice club, which had been assembled at a cost of millions. **Graeme went on to take over as manager at Stenhousemuir, leading them to their first promotion in the Ochilview club's history in 1999.**

Mark McGeown 1988–99

Mark McGeown's loyal work over 11 years in goal for Stirling Albion secured him their cult hero award. The keeper who was a dab hand at penalty saves attracted high praise from the fans. '**The best goalkeeper in the lower divisions in Scotland, probably the best part-time goalie in Britain. Pulled off unbelievable saves, including one very similar to Gordon Banks's famous save from Pele in the World Cup.**' While at Albion, Mark also appeared on Bruce Forsyth's *The Price is Right*. He ended up winning £30,000 worth of prizes, including a luxury holiday, a speedboat, pine bedroom furniture and an outdoor oven. However, he was then taken to court by a group claiming he had agreed to share the winnings with them. Mark eventually won the case, after four years, but it was a troubling time for all concerned. Mark was rewarded for his loyalty to Stirling with a testimonial against Rangers in 1998.

Kevin Francis 1991–95 & 2000

At six foot seven **Kevin Francis** was destined to make a big impression on the **Stockport** crowd when he joined from **Derby County** in the early **Nineties.** After a handful of games, he scored his first goal. It wasn't pretty and the fans were still to be convinced of his pedigree. However, he ended the season with five goals from 11 starts and helped the Hatters to escape from the bottom division for the first time in 21 years. The subsequent step up in class caused Kevin no problems. He paired up with Andy Preece and scored the goals that led County into two Wembley finals that season. Kevin scored in both legs against Burnley in the Autoglass Trophy Northern final, which took Stockport to their

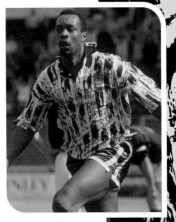

first ever Wembley final. They lost that final to Stoke. He also scored in the 2–1 play-off final defeat by Peterborough. The next campaign produced 28 goals, and the next few years saw two more Wembley appearances, but County sadly failed to break their duck at the home of football. Eventually Kevin moved to his hometown club Birmingham for £800,000, but not before coming on as a sub and scoring in his farewell appearance. He returned for a short spell in 2000 and has also been voted Stockport's Player of the Century.

Nominations Alun Armstrong Luke Beckett Kevin Francis

George Berry 1982–90

Does George Berry have the most magnificent hair of all our cult heroes? He's certainly got to be up there challenging for the best thatch in football with his memorable 'afro'. The man was a comedian and an extrovert whose antics endeared him to the City fans. They'd chant, **'Ooh Georgie Berry … Ooh Georgie Berry,'** and George would turn and blow them a kiss, unless of course he needed to keep his eyes on the ball. Then he'd wiggle his hips along to the song so that the crowd knew he appreciated their vocals. George wasn't perhaps the finest centre-half Stoke have ever had, but he would always give his all for the team. At half-time of his testimonial, played against neighbours Port Vale, George kissed the turf and then came and stood on the terraces for the second half. He adored the club. They adore him. He was also capped internationally for Wales on a handful of occasions.

Lex 'Lexy' Grant 1990–96

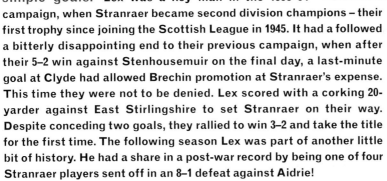

'Lex was the ultimate lower-league player. Overweight, lazy, glory-hunting – but incredibly talented. He could turn entire games if he was in the mood. He used to like chatting to the crowd too much to step up to the bigger leagues!' Lex was certainly very effective for Stranraer. He was really a goal-maker rather than a prolific scorer himself, but when he did score, it was rarely run of the mill: 'You never knew just what he was going to do. Lexy refused to score simple goals.' Lex was a key man in the 1993–94 campaign, when Stranraer became second division champions – their first trophy since joining the Scottish League in 1945. It had a followed a bitterly disappointing end to their previous campaign, when after their 5–2 win against Stenhousemuir on the final day, a last-minute goal at Clyde had allowed Brechin promotion at Stranraer's expense. This time they were not to be denied. Lex scored with a corking 20-yarder against East Stirlingshire to set Stranraer on their way. Despite conceding two goals, they rallied to win 3–2 and take the title for the first time. The following season Lex was part of another little bit of history. He had a share in a post-war record by being one of four Stranraer players sent off in an 8–1 defeat against Airdrie!

Gary Rowell 1975–84

Nominations John Kay Jim Montgomery **Gary Rowell**

Gary Rowell was brought up in Seaham as a staunch Sunderland fan. He made his debut in the 1975–76 season, in which the Black Cats won the second division championship. The next campaign saw them relegated, but Gary wasn't disheartened. He won England Under-21 honours and scored 18 goals for Sunderland in the 1977–78 season. But it was the following campaign that secured Gary a place in every Sunderland fan's heart. He scored 21 goals in all, but three of them were much more significant than any others. Sunderland were playing away at bitter rivals Newcastle, and Gary chose this stage to score his first hat-trick. 'The sweetest moment in my whole life! I would have happily fathered a child for Gary after that performance … and I'm a bloke from the North-East!' In 1980, Sunderland returned to the top flight and for the next four seasons Gary regularly scored goals that helped keep them there. Within that period Gary bagged another memorable hat-trick against Arsenal at Roker Park. He is one of only three post-war players to have scored more than 100 goals for Sunderland. The others are Len Shackleton and Kevin Phillips.

Ivor Allchurch 1947–58 & 1965–68

Ivor was known as 'the Golden Boy of Welsh football'. He had everything. Marvellous control, the ability to beat players at will and a talent for shooting that meant he was a threat wherever he was on the pitch. As well as being a magnificent footballer, he was also known as a true gentleman on and off the park. **'Ivor was truly wonderful. An inspiration to all who saw him. What he did with the ball and how he treated his opponents was simply remarkable.'** In 1958 Ivor joined Newcastle United for a fee of around £25,000. Seven years later he returned to the Vetch at the age of 35, and in his final three seasons he missed just 20 games. He was Swansea's top scorer in his last two campaigns. In all he netted 164 league goals in 445 games. He made 68 appearances for Wales. Ivor finished his career playing in the Welsh leagues and was still going at the age of 50.

Don Rogers 1962–72

Most Town fans believe the finest footballer ever to wear the Swindon shirt was their skilful winger Don Rogers. The fact that he is the celebrated figure at the heart of the club's greatest ever achievement just adds more weight to his position as Swindon Town's all-time cult hero. The day of reckoning came at Wembley in the League Cup final in 1969. Swindon's opponents were the mighty Arsenal, a team including Bob Wilson, Frank McLintock and George Graham. Arsenal complained of flu in the camp, and about the pitch being in a poor state after being trampled during Horse of the Year Show the previous week. But still they were two divisions above Swindon and surely must win. Arsenal went 1–0 down, but equalised in the second half, taking the game to extra time. Cometh the hour, cometh Don Rogers. Towards the end of the first period Swindon got a corner. It floated through to Don, who gracefully brought it down with his right foot and scored with his left. With the final seconds ticking by, Don burst out of his own half, ran the length of the pitch and then cunningly swerved past Bob Wilson to seal one of the greatest footballing shocks of all time.

Derek 'the Dude' Dawkins 1984–89

Mention the name **Derek Dawkins** to most football fans and they are likely to stare back at you blankly. Mention the name **Derek Dawkins** to the following **S**purs stars and they are likely to go a little red in the face and look at their shoes. **O**ssie **A**rdiles, **R**ay **C**lemence, **G**ary **M**abbutt and **C**hris **W**addle all suffered embarrassment at the hands of the player the fans knew as 'the **D**ude'. The date was 23 **S**eptember 1987. The place was the **W**est **C**ountry. The occasion was the first leg of the second round of the **L**eague **C**up. To make things worse for **T**ottenham, **T**orquay's manager was **S**purs' former defender **C**yril **K**nowles, the man who inspired the song 'Nice one **C**yril'. Three years earlier **D**erek had come to **T**orquay on a free transfer from **B**ournemouth. With just three minutes of the match to go, 'the **D**ude' found himself 15 yards out with the ball at his feet and **R**ay **C**lemence in his way. Without thinking he

headed fourth-division **T**orquay to a first-leg victory and turned himself into his team's all-time cult hero. **'The coolest man in Torquay for his effort, the goal against Spurs and his hair!'** Sadly for **T**orquay, they lost the second leg 3–0 at **W**hite **H**art **L**ane.

Paul Gascoigne 1988–92

When Gazza's eyes filled with tears as he was booked in the World Cup semi-finals of Italia '90, the nation fell hook, line and sinker for this player of unparallelled ability. He cried because he realised that if England won that game against West Germany he'd miss the final. However, for Spurs fans, the love affair had begun a couple of years earlier, when Paul had left his beloved Newcastle in a £2 million switch to White Hart Lane. He was magic to watch. Capable of dribbling past half a team, he could also thread passes through gaps most others couldn't even see. At Spurs he just kept on improving. And in the FA Cup of 1991 he was immense. Time and time again he would help drag his team through to the next round. He was playing with the country's finest marksman, Gary Lineker, a man who thrived on the opportunities Gazza could bring. And then there was the clowning. **Bobby Robson tagged Gazza 'daft as a brush,' so Gazza appeared with a brush poking out of his trousers.** He enjoyed his celebrity and once appeared in public wearing 'comedy breasts'. Paul loved to clown and he was good at it. He also drank too much and later had difficulties in his private life. But the Spurs fans adored him and the greatest single reason for them choosing Gazza as their cult hero was his performance in the FA Cup semi-final of 1991. Spurs were playing deadly North London rivals Arsenal – who were chasing a league and cup double. The game was held at Wembley because of an unprecedented demand for tickets, and there were doubts over Gazza's fitness. Not for long. A free-kick was given 35 yards out – too far, surely, to have a shot. Next thing, Gazza had run up and blasted the ball so hard and accurately that David Seaman couldn't stop it going into the net. Spurs fans don't forget moments like those. Two goals from Gary Lineker ensured Spurs won the game 3–1, which brought on an FA Cup final against Brian Clough's Nottingham Forest. There was so much hype before the game about Gazza. Within minutes he had gone in with an over-the-top challenge. **Then, after a quarter of an hour, the terrible moment came. Gazza lunged at Gary Charles, and was stretchered off having ruptured his cruciate ligament.** Spurs won the match 2–1. Gazza got a winner's medal, but he was out of the game for a year and was never the same player again. Subsequently he moved to Lazio. He also scored a wonderful goal against Scotland in Euro '96. But his time in Italy and then with Rangers, Middlesbrough and Everton never really did justice to his amazing early promise.

John Aldridge 1991–98

The Tranmere love affair started for John Aldridge at a reasonably late stage in his career, or so it seemed. At the age of 32 John moved to Prenton Park. You'd think they might have been expecting to squeeze a couple more years out of the old war-horse. **In fact over the next seven seasons he knocked in 164 goals for the club in just 272 starts. A** typically phenomenal strike rate for the striker who also did Oxford, Liverpool and Real Sociedad proud. In 1988 John Aldridge wrote the sort of history he'd prefer to forget when he became the first player to fail to score a penalty in an FA Cup final. Dave Beasant's save must have sparked a Wembley desire in John. As manager of Tranmere he took them to two consecutive FA Cup quarter-finals, starting in 2000. That season they also reached the Worthington Cup final, losing 2–1 to Leicester City. Perhaps the most memorable of the FA Cup runs was in 2001, when they beat neighbours Everton 3–0 at Goodison Park, came from 3–0 down to beat Southampton 4–3, and even gave Liverpool a scare in the quarter-final before eventually losing 4–2.

Jimmy Walker 1993–2004

Jimmy 'Whacker' Walker was a keeper who put in over a decade of loyal service in the Walsall goal. He signed on a free transfer from Notts County and made a memorable start to his Saddlers career. Memorable for everyone except for Jimmy! The game was against Gillingham and Jimmy excelled, keeping a clean sheet. But in the dying moments he got clattered by two opposition players, and when the physio asked him how he was he replied, 'Who are you?' His memory did return, and four more clean sheets in his next five games ensured that the Bescot faithful wouldn't be forgetting Jimmy in a hurry. At five foot eleven Jimmy was a few inches shorter than most other keepers, and many believed it was this that stopped him gaining international honours. **'"Whacker" will be best remembered for his spectacular shot-stopping, alongside his wicked sense of humour that got him into trouble with a few managers over the years! He dealt with promotion and relegation in the same fantastic manner.'**

Nominations Alan Buckley Chris Marsh Jimmy Walker

Walsall

Luther Blissett 1975–83, 1984–88 & 1991–93

Luther Blissett is **Watford's** all-time record goalscorer: in three spells and **415** games with the club he managed to net **158** goals. He is a legend for that feat alone, but he is also one of the pioneering black players in the country, becoming one of the first black footballers to represent England. **Luther's** sphere of influence has actually spread a

lot further than just north of London. **T**he name 'Luther Blissett' represents an Italian anarchist society and has become a term in the country for general anti-establishment behaviour. **Luther** spent a season with **AC** Milan. Later in the **Nineties** four young Italians were stopped for travelling without tickets on a tram in **Rome. W**hen asked their identities they all insisted they were called **Luther Blissett. T**hey later unsuccessfully claimed in court that 'a collective name does not need a ticket.' **T**he real **Luther** has no connection to the group. He went on to help coach his beloved **Hornets.**

Cyrille Regis 1977–84

Cyrille Regis was a powerful striker and a Midlands legend, having played for West Brom, Coventry, Villa and Wolves. At West Brom he played in a side that not only won matches but also entertained, putting a smile on the faces of their fans. Cyrille arrived from Hayes for £5,000 and went on to earn five caps for England. The Baggies fans loved his muscular commitment. **'Big Cyrille will always have a place in the hearts of true Baggies. Loads of memorable goals and his sheer power and skill were awesome.'** Cyrille scored a scorching long-range effort against Norwich City in 1982 that was subsequently voted goal of the season. But Cyrille maintains it was not his best ever: 'I scored one against Man City where I was further out. Took it from inside my half all the way and blasted it past Joe Corrigan. But the game wasn't televised, so nobody can see it now!'

Bobby Moore 1958–74

Most people know that **Bobby Moore** was one of the greatest defenders ever and that he captained England during their finest hour, winning the **World Cup** in 1966. But to West Ham fans he was even more than that – so much so that they have a stand named after him. Bobby played with his majestic style over 600 times for the club, was chosen as their player of the year in 1961, 1963, 1968 and 1970, and was runner-up on three more occasions. He was voted Footballer of the Year in 1964, the season he captained the **FA Cup**-winning side that beat Preston 3–2 in the final. The following year he led the Hammers to victory in the European Cup Winners' Cup. After the 1966 World Cup triumph he picked up the **BBC Sports Personality of the Year** award and the following year was awarded the **OBE**. Eventually, in 1974, Bobby left for Fulham, who lost to West Ham in the next year's **FA Cup** final. The East End fans still idolised him. **'If God had been a centre-half he'd be on the bench watching Mooro!'** In 1993 Bobby died as a result of bowel cancer at the age of 53. His wife Stephanie set up the **Bobby Moore Fund**, which has raised millions of pounds to help research into the disease. Even now Bobby is touching people's lives.

Roberto Martinez 1995–2001

The summer of 1995 brought about a remarkable happening in Wigan. The event is known as the arrival of the 'Three Amigos'. Roberto Martinez and Isidro Diaz arrived from FC Balaguer, while Jesus Seba was signed from Real Zaragoza. Spanish fever took over, and the Latics faithful started to proclaim, 'Jesus is a Wiganer!' But it was Roberto, or 'Bob', who captured the fans' imagination the most. **'He was a star, three moves ahead of the rest of the team, with amazing vision. No-one could control the ball like Bob. Spanish flags and sombreros appeared on the terraces and "Ole!" become the regular chant. Now if you've ever been to Wigan, you'll know that's quite a feat!'** Roberto also holds the distinction of becoming the first Spanish player to appear in the FA Cup when he was selected for the first-round tie with Runcorn in 1995.

Steve Bull 1986–99

You'll struggle to find a player anywhere who is worshipped as passionately as the **Wolves** fans idolise **Steve Bull**. 'He helped to cheer up the whole city during the Eighties and Nineties. When he got the ball people would already be celebrating a goal before he had even shot!' **Bully** was the ultimate no-nonsense striker and scored over 50 goals in a season on two occasions. He terrorised defenders with his direct style and unstoppable commitment. Remarkably, **Steve** made it into **Bobby Robson's England** squad that came so close to winning the **World Cup** in Italy in 1990. He was a striker playing outside the top flight, but **Robson** knew that world-class defenders would never have come up against a centre-forward quite like **Steve Bull**. Although he came close he never did reach the top division with **Wolves**, but when the club were eventually promoted to the **Premiership** in 2003, every **Black Country** fan had a smile across their face and the thought of '**Bully**' in their mind.

Wrexham

Joey Jones's clenched fist salute is famous in Wrexham. He first had the opportunity to use his trademark celebration with the club when he made his first-team debut at the tender age of 17. Joey immediately established himself as the first-team right-back, and in the 1973–74 season he was a valuable part of the side that reached the quarter-finals of the FA Cup for the first time in the club's history. Along the way they beat Crystal Palace and Middlesbrough, as well as Southampton, before going out to Burnley in the days when they were in the top flight. Joey then went on to win his first domestic honour in 1975, when Wrexham beat Cardiff City to win the Welsh Cup final. Before he could make his debut in European football, Joey

was sold to Liverpool for £110,000. Joey had supported the Anfield club as a boy and he went on to win two league championships and the European Cup before a club record fee of £210,000 brought him back to the Racecourse Ground. He left again, this time for Chelsea, only to return, now as a centre-back, as Wrexham battled in the fourth division. From 1989 Joey took on coaching duties with the club, and by the time he retired from playing, he had won 72 caps for Wales.

Nominations Gary Bennett **Joey Jones** Mickey Thomas

Steve Brown 1994–2004

Steve Brown set up his own website in his testimonial year and used it to thank the fans for helping to drive him on during his Wycombe career. Steve found it quite difficult in his first season even though the club were promoted to the second division. However, in the next campaign he found his feet and was voted Wycombe's player of the season. The tireless midfielder played for several managers in his time at Wanderers. They included Martin O'Neill and John Gregory, but it was under Lawrie Sanchez that Steve and the club captured the public's imagination. The year was 2001 and in the fifth round of the FA Cup Wycombe drew Sanchez's old club Wimbledon. Twice they went behind, and their keeper saved a penalty, but somehow they managed to hang in there. The score was 2–2 after extra time. In a nail-biting shoot-out Wycombe won 8–7 on penalties. In the quarter-final Wanderers beat Leicester City, which meant a semi-final against Liverpool. Steve and the side couldn't quite complete the dream, losing 2–1, but the fans appreciate the contribution made by Steve Brown.

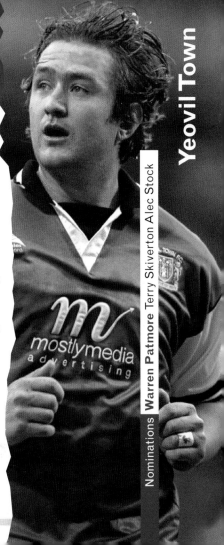

Yeovil Town

Nominations Warren Patmore Terry Skiverton Alec Stock

Warren Patmore was a big, burly centre-forward who scored goals galore for the Glovers in the non-league divisions. He made an explosive start. A month after joining from Northern Irish club Ards, Warren helped himself to all four Yeovil goals in a win over Walton and Hersham. **That first season brought 27 goals in all and saw Warren win over the Huish Park crowd.** The following season was even more of a success. Another hat-trick in a 6–0 FA Cup win over Backwell United was followed by a storming campaign that ended with Yeovil taking the Isthmian League title and Warren bagging 29 goals. In his third season at Yeovil 'Wazza' was sporadically used as a central defender. He was proving as handy at stopping goals as he was at scoring them. By the time Warren moved into season four he was chasing 100 goals for the club. It was a header against Leek Town that brought up Warren's century. He then ran 90 yards to celebrate with his adoring fans. That season he also gained his first cap and goal for England's non-league international side. In Warren's final season at Yeovil, the club finished runners-up in the Conference. At this point he moved to Rushden & Diamonds, where Warren claimed the distinction of scoring the Northamptonshire club's first goal in the Football League.

Cult Heroes XI

This is a Football Focus stab at an all-time cult hero eleven. It's designed to prompt some debate as the programme will soon be searching for your favourite cult side. Please email us at *football@bbc.co.uk* with your suggested team and give the reasons behind your line-up. Remember *Football Focus* is on every Saturday during the season on **BBC1** at **12.10 p.m.**

Admittedly we've not been too rigid with the footballing formation, but I think every cult team should have a burly goalkeeper with the bulk to snap a goal-post in half should the going get tough. Hence Grenville Millington between the sticks. At right-back I've got a comedian, Charlie Williams, to keep spirits up. Lindsay 'Wolfie' Smith can hoof long clearances with accuracy and has the look of a porn star to allow us to play sexy football. George Berry provides the biggest hair, and Derek Dawkins is simply 'the Dude'. In midfield we have a blend of quality and deviance. Stan Bowles gives us flamboyant skills along with unpredictable gambling tips. Gazza can dazzle while wearing 'comedy breasts'. The late Robin Friday sticks two fingers up to anyone who questions his ability, and 'Vodka Vic' Kasule can hit the ball almost as hard as he hits the bottle. Up front we have the ultimate one-club hero, able to eat kebabs and still deliver on a Saturday, Matt Le Tissier. To cap it all, perhaps the greatest cult icon ever, womaniser, boozer, yet still Pele's choice as the greatest footballer ever, Georgie Best.

George Best
(Manchester United)

Matt Le Tissier
(Southampton)

Stan Bowles
(Queens Park Rangers)

Paul 'Gazza' Gascoigne
(Tottenham Hotspur)

Robin Friday
(Cardiff City & Reading)

'Vodka Vic' Kasule
(Albion Rovers)

**Derek 'the Dude'
Dawkins**
(Torquay United)

Lindsay 'Wolfie' Smith
(Cambridge United)

George Berry
(Stoke City)

Charlie Williams
(Doncaster Rovers)

Grenville Millington
(Chester City)

Picture Credits

BBC Worldwide would like to thank those who provided photographs and permission to reproduce copyright material. While every effort has been made to trace and acknowledge all copyright holders, we would like to apologize should there have been any errors or omissions.

All pictures have been supplied by Action Images, except those provided by the following:
Airdrie and Coatbridge Advertiser 11, 159; *Alloa Advertiser* 12; John D. Cross 23; Ronnie McAllister 28; Burnley Football Club 34; *Bury Times* 35; Western Mail & Echo Ltd 37; *Chester Chronicle* 45, 159; Clyde Football Club 47; West Dunbartonshire Libraries 57; Fife Council Museums: Methil Heritage Centre 61; *The Northern Scot* 63; Angus County Press Ltd 66; Cumbrian Newspapers Ltd 69; Mail Publications Ltd 76; Kidderminster Harriers 80; *Manchester Chad* 94; Montrose FC 98; Pete Norton 102; Aberdeen Journals 111; Ian Black 116; The *Herald & Evening Times* picture archive 117; *Reading Evening Post* 122, 159; Norma and Reg Jenkins 123; Andrew Allan Photography 124; Stranraer Football Club 141; Dick Mattick 144; Torbay News Agency 145, 159; Empics 46, 106, 143; SNS Group 18, 20, 62, 77, 99 & 109.